MOROCCO

Ken Bernstein
and
Michel Puysségur

JPMGUIDES

appealing crafts

CONTENTS

3	This Way Morocco
7	Flashback
13	On the Scene
13	Capitals
19	North Coast
25	Imperial Heart
33	Marrakesh
49	Resorts
55	The South
63	Oases and Desert
71	Shopping
75	Dining Out
78	Sports
80	The Hard Facts
96	Index

Features
68 Understanding Morocco

Maps
86 Agadir
88 Casablanca
89 Essaouira
90 Fez
91 Meknes
92 Marrakesh
94 Rabat
95 Tangier

Fold-out map
Morocco
Southern Morocco

life in the desert

a warm welcome

tasty cuisine

THIS WAY MOROCCO

Some place-names incite dreams. Just to pronounce Katmandu or Mandalay can put a faraway look into a traveller's eyes. So it is with Marrakesh. Could the city really be as exotic, as engrossing, as unforgettable as its centuries-old reputation implies? You bet it could, even without the snake charmers and acrobats.

Flight of Imagination

In Morocco all the cities seem to have evocative names. Think of Fez, Meknès and Tangier. In fact, you need hardly go beyond the nation's metropolis, Casablanca, to shift the imagination into high gear. Bogart is long gone, but it might as well be the 1940s in the hubbub of spice vendors, fish stalls and second-hand clothing merchants operating in the medina just around the corner from the new luxury hotels.

And consider the storied names of the country's most remarkable physical features: the Rif mountains, the Atlas mountains, and the Sahara desert. Even the map won't let you forget that this is no prosaic place.

Coast to Coast

An ocean and a sea—the Atlantic and the Mediterranean—link Morocco to other continents, and incidentally provide refreshing breezes, outstanding beaches and memorable seafood dinners. With few exceptions, though, the "real" Morocco is inland: lonely mountain villages, cities built of mud, pervaded with medieval atmosphere, and the beauties and mysteries of the desert.

With an area of more than 710,000 sq km (nearly 275,000 sq miles), Morocco is bigger than Texas. (The official area includes disputed Saharan territories.) The capital of the kingdom is Rabat on the Atlantic coast, with a population of 2 million. In a country that can grow tomatoes and dates at the same time, there is room enough for a great diversity in culture as well as climate. The California-style skyscrapers of Casablanca are a world away from the ochre kasbahs of the desert. Even within a single city, cultures collide. Donkeys go where taxis cannot pass, and a veiled traditionalist, hiding all her charms except the eyes, shops alongside young women in knee-length skirts.

The road signs are in Arabic and French. For historical reasons Spanish is the best-known foreign language of the north; elsewhere fluent French is heard. Among themselves the population speaks Arabic (the official language) and Berber (colloquially), depending on the region

The biggest mosque.
Until modern times the immense, ancient Karaouine Mosque in Fez was the largest in Morocco. Now it has been overtaken by Casablanca's **King Hassan II Mosque**, a colossal statement of faith rising just above the Atlantic waves. Laser lighting effects crown its minaret, visible for miles around, with a sort of celestial cloud.

Author's Image

and the situation. Everyone drinks mint tea, most visibly the gregarious men of all ages, idling away so many hours in the cafés.

A Glass of Tea

You may find yourself taking mint tea as the guest of a carpet merchant or a jewellery shop owner. The preparation, pouring and sipping of the refreshing beverage can be almost as meticulously mannered as the Japanese tea ceremony. Not only does the gesture reflect traditional Moroccan hospitality; it may also, by no coincidence, help persuade you to buy something.

If you hate haggling, try to make it a game—always a smile, always keeping in mind that the seller won't lose, no matter how fiercely you think you are bargaining. Just don't say "maybe" if you really mean "no".

Shopping in Morocco starts with morocco—the fine, soft leather that has taken the country's name for centuries, as in morocco-bound books. Less celebrated leather turns up in every souk in every form from suitcases to camel saddles. After you've bought a pair of slippers, you may want to go all the way and acquire a kaftan or a jellaba. As well as necklaces, trays of beaten copper and brassware—and the carpet that caught your eye at the outset.

The Choices

Morocco can be as strenuous as you want to make it. Mount a camel—a one-humped dromedary, to be exact—to have your picture taken, or lope off for a week-long Sahara safari from oasis to oasis. Admire the Atlas mountains from a palm grove in the desert, or climb Mount Toubkal, at 4,167 m (13,672 ft) the highest peak in North Africa. Lounge on a beach or build some muscles fighting the waves and the breeze on a sailboard.

On land or sea, the sporting possibilities are extravagant. You can water-ski in the Mediterranean or ski down the snowy slopes only an hour away from the poolside in Marrakesh. Trout fishermen go to the rivers, bass and perch anglers take to Morocco's lakes, and for everything up to shark and blue fin tuna, the ocean awaits. Golf and polo fit for a king and tennis galore keep landlubber sportsmen out of mischief.

After Sunset

When the breeze begins to rustle the palm fronds and the muezzin chants his call to early evening prayer, it's time to abandon the swimming pool and think about the hours ahead. Moroccans, 99 per cent of them Muslims, tend to avoid alcohol, but they are tolerant of the tastes of strangers, so

istockphoto.com/Rotthaus

The Moroccan art of ceramic ornament is not mosaic but *zellige*.

the hotel barmen can mix up any cocktail you may fancy. Wine is produced more than competently in Morocco, and you'll have no problem finding a suitable vintage to accompany your dinner. The national cuisine ranges from homely, spicy standbys to the most exquisite delicacies.

After dinner you may want to investigate the music of the country and study the applied art of belly dancing, or work off some calories in a club. Whatever your choice, it's a perfect contrast to the day's adventures.

Storks put the ancient Roman columns of Volubilis to good use.

FLASHBACK

In the beginning the Sahara was nothing like the ocean of sand that awes us today. Until only a few thousand years ago it was fertile enough to support the kind of animals featured in southern African safaris, from elephants to zebras.

When it all dried up, primitive farmers turned into nomads, among them the first Moroccans. In some ways the Berbers are about as mysterious now as they ever were. They speak hundreds of local dialects throughout Africa, and, though fiercely independent, they have never formed a nation of their own.

The Phoenician Connection

Recorded history starts around 1000 BC when Phoenician traders opened a branch office at what is now the enclave of Melilla, on the Mediterranean coast. The Carthaginians, who eventually took over the Phoenician business, expanded commercial operations as far as Lixus (Larache), on the Atlantic. Carthaginian inscriptions have been unearthed inland, too, at Volubilis, near Meknès. After winning the Punic Wars, the Roman empire brutally erased Carthage from the map in 146 BC, though the word didn't reach far-flung colonies for years.

Mauretania Tingitana

The Romans developed North Africa as their bread basket. Eager administrators, they split it into four provinces; Morocco and Algeria were combined as *Mauretania Tingitana*—named after Tingis, now Tangier. Tingis won the rank of full-scale Roman city in 38 BC. One name shines from the archives of that epoch. The handsome, intellectual King Juba II of Mauretania, a Berber by birth, won the hand of Cleopatra Selene, thus becoming the son-in-law of Antony and Cleopatra. Alas, the saga ended unhappily. Around AD 40 the son of Juba and Cleo, Ptolemy, made a bad impression on the moody emperor Caligula, who ordered that the lad be executed.

Christians and Jews

The Romans had a hard time pacifying the Berbers and never ventured very far south, Rabat being their farthest-flung settlement. From Rome, Christianity spread through the empire, and by the 3rd century Morocco had four bishoprics. (There was also a significant Jewish culture, the result of migrations after the fall of Jerusalem in AD 70. The Jewish traditions, often combined with Berber customs, have been part of the Moroccan scene into modern times.) But the Roman empire was in free-fall decline and Morocco suffered the fringe of the Vandal unpleasantness that afflicted the Europe of the Dark Ages, in addition to wars, insurrections and all-round confusion.

The Islamic Tide

Early in the 7th century in the Arabian city of Mecca, the Prophet, Mohammed, heard a divine message and set it down in the Koran. Within a century of Mohammed's death in 632, the new religion had raced across Arabia and conquered hearts and minds all over the Middle East and North Africa.

Despatched from Damascus, the first Arab invaders sliced into Morocco in 682. They were led by Uqba Ibn Nafi, a dauntless general who went as far as he could go—overland to the Atlantic ocean at Agadir. Although he took key hostages to encourage the Berber tribes to convert, the Islamization of Morocco wasn't as quick and spontaneous as he might have hoped.

Into Spain

Northern Morocco, under Arab control early in the 8th century, was the embarkation point for the Moorish invasion of Europe. Tough Berber troops, newly converted to Islam, spearheaded the amphibious attack on Gibraltar in 711. Spain turned out to be a walkover for the invaders, who within a few years had conquered almost all the territory up to the Pyrenees. The capital of Muslim-occupied Spain, established in Córdoba, became one of the world's biggest, most beautiful and refined cities.

The Reconquest of Spain by the Christian forces seesawed for nearly eight centuries.

The First Dynasty

Back in Morocco, a great-grandson of the Prophet arrived towards the end of the 8th century to inspire the faithful and set the stage for an Arab kingdom. Moulay Idris reigned but briefly from the old Roman city of Volubilis before he was poisoned and assassinated; his memory is revered in the nearby hill town named after him. The dynasty he founded went on to considerable achievements. Moulay's heir, Idris II, set up his capital at Fez. The city's greatness was soon spurred by the arrival of devout, skilled workers from Córdoba and Tunisia's religious centre,

Kairouan. You could say that Idris I and II were the founding fathers of Morocco.

The Almoravids

It lasted less than a century, but the Almoravid dynasty unified the country and spread Morocco's power as far as Algiers and Andalusia. The Almoravids were nomadic Berbers from the desert of what is now Mauritania, as ascetic and devout as the toughest, most puritanical warrior-monks. They forced their standards on the people and built a fortress at Marrakesh. As time passed, the Almoravids were softened by the civilization that surrounded them, as well as the influence of the Spanish branch of the family. Art began to flourish in Morocco, and one of the most magnificent mosques in all Islam, the Karaouine mosque, brought splendour to Fez. On the military front, Emir Yusuf ibn Tashfin took up the struggle for Islam in Spain and won a crucial victory over King Alfonso VI of Castile in 1086.

The Almohads

Early in the 12th century another Berber dynasty, the fervent Al-

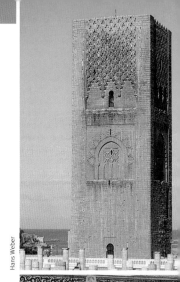

Rabat's Hassan Tower looms over ruins of the vast 12th-century mosque. | One of the monumental gateways of Fez.

Hans Weber

mohads, took power and quickly propelled Morocco to imperial greatness. Before their era waned, nearly 150 years later, they ruled over all of North Africa and much of southern Spain. An Almohad sultan, Yacoub el Mansour, won a big battle in Spain in 1195, then devoted himself to embellishing his reign. He built a new capital in Rabat and sponsored the exquisite minarets of Marrakesh and Seville.

In science, engineering, architecture, art and all-round culture the Almohads presided over the most brilliant chapter of the golden age.

Setbacks

The Merinid dynasty, headquartered in a flourishing Fez, continued the cultural and artistic achievements of the Almohads while suffering battlefield reverses. Among their greatest successes was building the fabulous Alhambra complex in Granada. However, soon only Granada kept faith in a Spain that had been all but recaptured by the Christians. As if the Spanish situation wasn't difficult enough, the Portuguese began raids on the Moroccan coast.

Less than 30 years after the Merinids had been ousted, Granada, too, finally surrendered—to the "Catholic monarchs", Ferdinand and Isabella. Muslims and Jews expelled from the Spain of the Inquisition rushed to asylum in Morocco.

The Saadians

The Saadian dynasty reversed a trend of military setbacks in the 16th century, ousting the Portuguese from some, though not all, of their Moroccan footholds. The wily, expansionist Ahmad al-Mansur won glory by capturing Timbuktu and bringing back slaves and gold.

Under the Saadians, corsairs ran a profitable privateering industry from Moroccan ports, part of the lurid era of the Barbary (from "Berber") pirates.

Moulay Ismaïl

A larger than life sultan, Moulay Ismaïl, who reigned as a very effective tyrant from 1672 to 1727, chalked up numerous successes in military and diplomatic affairs. He ousted European expansionists from most of their Moroccan beachheads and kept the Turks at bay. His greatest monument is the palatial city of Meknès, where he is buried. The far-sighted Moulay Ismaïl was an early monarch of the Alaouite dynasty, which claimed descent from the Prophet.

Through thick and thin the dynasty has shown exceptional longevity; the King Mohammed VI is the latest of the line.

"Protectorate"

French, Spanish and to a lesser degree German interests became ever more forceful early in the 20th century. After their initial economic penetration the Europeans began nibbling away territory—France took Casablanca, Spain occupied historic Ksar el Kabir, south of Tangier. (Spain had held enclaves on the north coast for centuries: Melilla and Ceuta are still Spanish External Provinces.)

In 1912 an economically vulnerable Morocco agreed to the Treaty of Fez establishing a Franco-Spanish "protectorate". When Berbers in the Rif mountains rebelled in the 1920s, France and Spain sent in hundreds of thousands of troops to restore control.

Towards Independence

Demands for Moroccan independence, coordinated by the new Istiqlal party, surfaced during World War II. The sultan, Mohammed V, sympathized, at first silently, and then with words and actions, and finally the French lost patience. The sultan was deposed in 1953, exiled to Madagascar. By the time he returned triumphantly to Morocco two years later, the struggle had almost been won.

Independence was signed and sealed in 1956; Mohammed V ruled as a popular king until his tragic death after a minor operation in 1961.

A New Dynasty

By the time Hassan II assumed the throne, his whole life had been a training course for the political and religious leadership of his country. As crown prince he had been educated in both Arabic and French. His rather authoritarian reign would survive economic strains, political unrest, a failed coup and an assassination attempt. He died of a heart attack in July 1999 and was succeeded by his son, enthroned on July 30 as Mohammed VI at the age of 36 He soon set the country on the road to democracy and granted more power to women. He is a popular king though has sometimes angered fundamentalists; his arrival at the head of the country marks the entry of Morocco into the 21st century.

Frontiers of the Future

Morocco's territory was greatly enlarged in 1976 after the dramatic Green March of thousands of citizens to the western Sahara. The ultimate details of the borders are yet to be decided, under the aegis of the UN. Meanwhile, Morocco is developing the mineral-rich territory whose capital, Laayoune, has bloomed. Oil has been discovered offshore.

Bathed in a serene light, the prayer room of
Hassan II Mosque in Casablanca.

Huber/Sclarandis

ON THE SCENE

The most popular sightseeing itineraries start with the imperial cities or Marrakesh. Other programmes go from north to south, from the Mediterranean to the Sahara. And some sun-lovers never get beyond the beach at Agadir. This guide divides the essentials into six sectors, starting with the country's first and second largest cities—the capitals of industry and politics, less than 100 km (62 miles) apart, and ending with a section on the desert and oases.

Capitals

The cities of Casablanca and Rabat are fairly close together but both have international airports. Going from one city centre to the other takes less than an hour on the commuter train, a bit more on the motorway. Utterly different, the two make a fine match: "Casa" for its enthusiasm and commercial power, Rabat for history, space and grace.

Casablanca

About one in ten of all Moroccans lives in Casablanca. Almost everything dates from the 20th century, most winningly in the newest areas of the city centre, shining with contemporary architecture and comfortable wealth. Palm trees eight storeys tall line the boulevards, which are interspersed with shady parks containing outdoor cafés and ice-cream shops.

Grand Hassan II Mosque

You can't miss the "new beacon of Islam" on the Atlantic shore of Casablanca. The country's tallest structure, the minaret is nearly 200 m (655 ft) high. It dominates the skyline from land and sea, day and (especially) night, when it is dramatically lit and the laser beam on top illuminates the way to Mecca. The Mega-Mosque, as it has been nicknamed, is the biggest anywhere outside of Mecca: its prayer hall is the size of four football fields, and an overflow crowd of 80,000 additional faithful can easily be accommodated on the esplanade outside. All the auxiliary facilities, from *medersa* (religious school) to underground garages, are on a similar superlative scale. The architect, Michel Pinseau, is French; thousands of Moroccan artisans produced the impressive details of a monument that imposes spirituality on the bustling commercial city.

Colonial City

When the French landed in Casablanca in 1907 the population was scarcely 20,000. The spacious colonial city they built is criss-crossed by stately boulevards and centred on the square called Place des Nations Unies. A grand municipal ensemble combines European and Moorish architectural elements in a style referred to as Mauresque. The planners crowned the arcaded city hall with the sort of clock tower that would be more suitable on a railway station.

An attractive vestige of the colonial era, the **Cathédrale du Sacré Cœur** has been deconsecrated and is now used as a school, but its uplifting design still adds to Casablanca's attractions. Several smaller churches serve the local Christian community.

Old Medina

Once you're inside the old walled city, it's self-explanatory. The medina is small enough to ensure that you don't get seriously lost, the streets are relatively wide and bright, the salesmen on the whole no more grasping than a friendly shoal of octopuses. If you're not in the market for a second-hand watch or a slightly used radio, just spend some time browsing among the alluring food and spice stalls.

New Medina

In the southeast part of town in the Habbous district, the new medina was built by the French in the 1930s. With the streets laid out in straight, neat rows, it is a tidied-up, "improved" version of traditional architecture.

Aïn Diab

The other side of big-city life is out beyond the port, the old medina and the titanic Hassan II mosque, in the suburb of Aïn Diab. You can walk there; it isn't too far, or take a taxi or the bus.

The corniche road leads to a string of luxurious hotels, clubs and resorts on the ocean. This is where Casablanca people go in summer to escape the heat, eat seafood, have a swim (probably in a sea-water pool) and meet friends.

Tricky tides grip the Atlantic here, and the water is hardly clean and pure, but Aïn Diab is worth a look, and a breath of sea air.

Rabat

The French can take credit for transforming it into a worthy capital, but Rabat, sited where the Bou Regreg River meets the Atlantic, has been a significant city since the time of the Romans. The most remarkable monuments on view today reflect achievements from early medieval times to the present. One of the most striking juxtapositions anywhere is the 12th-century Hassan Tower next door to the 1970s mausoleum of Mohammed V.

The Medina

This is surely the perfect medina for beginners. Unlike the puzzling mazes of some other cities,

Claude Hervé-Bazin

istockphoto.com/Franklin

Huber/Morandi

Water sellers wear a traditional costume to ply their trade. | Intricately sculpted marble on the mausoleum of Mohammed V. | Kasbah des Oudaïas seen from the Bou Regreg river.

Rabat's old town follows a tidy grid pattern of straight streets where it's fairly difficult to lose your way. Another advantage: the merchants are so low-key they wouldn't hassle a fly. But there's no shortage of local colour. Just inside the gate, public scribes with typewriters fill in forms for illiterate or unsure clients. Here, too, lurk artisans in hope of work—house-painters with their rollers and brushes, masons with their trowels. The supply far exceeds the demand. There are also beggars with every imaginable disability, and some you could never have imagined.

The shopping includes silk embroidery, jewellery, brightly coloured Rabat carpets, copperware, and leather.

Kasbah des Oudaïas

Just north (and uphill) from the medina, the lived-in kasbah is an atmospheric zone in which to wander, but you should be wary of would-be guides who don't hesitate to point non-clients in the wrong direction.

The main entrance to the enclave is through **Bab al-Kasbah**, otherwise called the Oudaïa gate, a glorious example of decorative stone-carving from the end of the 12th century. The kasbah's main street leads past iron-studded house doors and the oldest mosque in Rabat to the open cannon-and-semaphore platform, with views over the ocean, the river and the town of Salé on the opposite bank.

Another vantage point nearby is a shaded outdoor café in a cool and restful Andalusian-style garden. A stairway climbs from here to a restored 17th-century palace, which houses the **Museum of Moroccan Arts**. It features all national crafts from polychrome pottery and Berber jewellery to local carpets.

The Mausoleum

Mounted soldiers in theatrical red uniforms maintain a vigil at the entrance to the complex containing the tombs of Mohammed V and his son Hassan II, and the adjacent ruins of a mosque from the Almohad era. The mausoleum itself is protected by a guard of honour of dismounted troops; the changing of the guard is not

---

Impressive Roman ruins. The Romans colonized as far afield as Rabat, but the most impressive ruins are **Volubilis,** near Meknès, and **Lixus,** near Larache. The Volubilis site, dominating a magnificent plateau, is so big that coach loads of tourists don't impinge on each other. The Lixus ruins evoke the legends of Hercules and civilizations of Carthage as well as Rome.

quite in the Buckingham Palace precision league but definitely worth a picture.

All the traditional Moroccan arts and materials have been used in the modern mausoleum—tile, marble, precious stones and brass worked to perfection. Unusually, non-Muslims are permitted inside, to look down on the tombs of the two kings.

Hassan Tower

The Hassan Mosque was an ambitious 12th-century project, abandoned on the death of the expansionist sultan Yacoub el Mansour. The size of the mosque can be gauged from the forest of stumps of columns arrayed here. The monument left standing tall must be one of the most beautiful minarets anywhere. The Hassan Tower dates from the same time and displays the same inspiration as the Giralda in Seville and the Koutoubia minaret in Marrakesh.

Archaeological Museum

Cats and kittens cavort playfully in the patio of the Archaeological Museum, in the new town. The main exhibition covers a bit of everything ancient, from the most primitive stones of prehistoric times to oil lamps, jewellery and coins, and early Islamic-era pottery. But the museum's most valuable possessions are kept in the annexe, labelled the Bronze Collection. The star attraction is a beautiful sculpture showing the Berber features of King Juba II, excavated at Volubilis.

Chellah

The necropolis of the Merinid dynasty, a fortress called the Chellah, was built in the 14th century on the site of the Roman colony of Sala. Ruins of a Roman forum, a temple, shops and baths have been unearthed within the walls. Notwithstanding the scattering of royal tombs and a roofless mosque with a crumbled minaret, the Chellah remains a cheerful place to visit. A lovely tropical garden makes all the difference.

Salé

Named after the Roman Sala, the walled city of Salé was founded in the 11th century. You can get there by bus, *grand-taxi* or rowing boat. In the Middle Ages, sailboats reached the town along a long-lost channel reaching the giant gate called Bab el Mrisa. Religious monuments are the main "official" sights—the Almohad Grand Mosque (the interior is off limits to non-Muslims) and the spacious Merinid-era *medersa*, decorated with ceramic tiles and carved screens. "Unofficially", the medina, unspoiled, is off the tourist track, and the souks are absorbingly colourful.

Earnest discussion in one of the cafés of the Petit Socco.

hemis.fr/Boisvieux

North Coast

It's only 13 km (8 miles) from Tangier to Spain, so close you can almost hear the wail of a flamenco singer wafting across the Strait of Gibraltar. At the crossroads of the Atlantic and the Mediterranean, this northern coast of Morocco has a chequered history and a cosmopolitan appeal.

Tangier

International intrigue, smugglers, refugees, eccentric or disreputable characters: the tolerant people of Tangier, who cheerfully call themselves Tangerines, have seen it all. Three thousand years ago the Phoenicians set up a trading post and fishing port here. Later it became the Roman town of Tingis. Arab rulers arrived in the 8th century, and Portugal captured the city in the 15th. For a time it belonged to Charles II of England. In 1906 the city came under the control of eight European powers while Spain ruled the rest of the North. Which is why your school Spanish will take you far in Tangier and northern Morocco.

Grand Socco

Just outside the old town walls, the Grand Socco (big souk) is one of the traditional centres of Tangier life. From here you walk through an archway into the medina, a bustling hillside of winding streets and lanes in which artisans of different trades congregate.

Petit Socco

In the heart of the medina, the Petit Socco (little souk) is a pleasant open space with several cafés. It used to be a crossroads of intrigue in the Gateway to Africa. All Tangier still passes here — businessmen in striped jellabas, women in kaftans or Paris dresses, and a mischievous cast of children.

Kasbah

At the top of the hill above the medina, the kasbah seems impregnable from land or sea. This fortress was the centre of administration of old Tangier, where Moulay Ismail chose to build his palace behind the batteries of cannon installed on the walls. The **Sultan's Garden**, part of Moulay Ismail's 17th-century palace, is just beyond a large unmarked doorway in Rue Riad Sultan.

Museum of Moroccan Arts

From the fragrant garden you enter the sultan's palace, Dar el Makhzen. Its museum covers all manner of treasures, from illuminated Korans to wood and metal work, as well as Berber carpets and a collection of ceramics. The adjoining **Antiquities Museum** goes

hemis.fr/Frances

Bernard Joliat

Huber/Spila

back as far as Stone Age finds and Roman mosaics. With its two richly decorated courtyards, the palace itself is a work of art.

Forbes Museum of Military Miniatures
The unconventional American magazine publisher Malcolm Forbes, remembered for motor-cycle-riding and party-giving, maintained a residence in the Mendoub Palace in Rue Shake-speare. He died in 1990 and left a record-breaking collection of toy soldiers, many deployed to illustrate notable battles.

New Town
Leading south from the Grand Socco, the Rue de la Liberté goes to the heart of the modern city of Tangier—Place de France and Boulevard Pasteur. Cafés, restaurants, travel agencies and book-stores are all within a few streets, and there's a fine panorama of the harbour and the Spanish main-land from the terrace.

Cap Spartel
A few miles due west of Tangier, an old lighthouse stares out at all

A line-up of dishes and tajines for cous-cous. | The festival at Asilah ends with a fantasia, horsemen galloping, rifles firing into the sky. | A henna tatoo makes an ephemeral souvenir.

the supertankers sailing between the Atlantic and the Mediterranean. You can climb the spiral staircase to the observation level and celebrate the superlative: Cap Spartel is the northwesternmost point in Africa. Robinson beach is an inviting, endless expanse of sand but the tides make it risky for swimmers. Down the coast, prehistoric people quarried stone in the Caves of Hercules. The mythological hero Hercules, or Heracles, is a household name hereabouts, for his labours were said to have created the Strait of Gibraltar.

Tetouan

Echoes of Andalusia account for the charm of Tetouan, a skyline of whitewashed houses on the slopes of the Rif mountains overlooking the Mediterranean. The city traces its history back more than 2,000 years, but the modern phase began at the end of the 15th century when Muslim and Jewish refugees from the Christian Reconquest of Spain flooded in. They brought with them the skills of Andalusian architects, artists and artisans.

Place Hassan II

The thoroughly modern ceremonial square of Tetouan is a wide open space bordered by palm trees, flag-poles and tiled minaret-like towers; the paving inter-

Shun the hustlers. Most tourist areas in Morocco are afflicted with unofficial guides, freelance shopping advisers, confidence tricksters and aggressive hawkers. Tangier is perhaps the national capital of hustlers; they seem to speak a little of every language on earth, and they aim to separate you from some—if not all—of your money. Learning how to say "no" with a smile is part of your education. If you need a genuine guide, go to the tourist office.

Huber/Giocoso

weaves geometric forms. It's all a startling departure from the typical traditional Moroccan square. The restored Royal Palace occupies one end.

The Medina

Fine Andalusian touches such as wrought-iron balconies and colourful tile decorations make this the ultimate Mauresque medina of Morocco. In the souks, Tetouan's shopping temptations, from

Moroccan doors have been painted blue since time immemorial.

textiles to pottery to contraband from the nearby Spanish enclave of Ceuta, ambush the visitor at every turning.

Chaouen

Red-tile roofs and whitewashed walls distinguish the small mountain town of Chaouen, also known as Chefchaouen or Xauen, founded in the 15th century. Isolated for hundreds of years, the inhabitants maintained their Andalusian architecture, gardens and handicrafts. There are two main squares: Place Outa el Hammam, next to the kasbah, and the more formal, fountained Place El Makhzen. Plunge into Chaouen's souks and immerse yourself in the animation, the sounds and aromas of this singular town.

Asilah

An hour's drive down the Atlantic coast from Tangier, the fishing port of Asilah has a distinctive sort of charm, celebrated only in recent years with the inauguration of an international cultural festival. Asilah has been around since Phoenician days but the dominant influence visible today comes from the Portuguese, who fortified the town in the 15th and 16th centuries. The roomy but labyrinthine streets of the medina are easily explored, with ramparts and towers as reminders of the days of derring-do. In the early 20th century a notorious brigand named Raisuli had a palace built overlooking the sea. It figures in the international festival in August. Other attractions are a long beach and some relaxed seafood restaurants whose reputation spreads as far as Tangier.

Lixus

Just north of the quiet port of Larache, Lixus was an important colony of ancient Rome, with much evidence to prove it. On the site you can inspect the remains of an acropolis, temples, an amphitheatre, and in the lower town, salt and fish-sauce factories. Legend places the Garden of Hesperides alongside the river Loukos at Lixus. Here Hercules would have stolen golden apples as the penultimate challenge on his way to Mount Olympus.

Enclaves. Since the 15th and 16th centuries, two Spanish possessions have been clinging to the northern coast of Morocco. Ceuta and Melilla both have Spanish military bases, *paradores*, brandy and sherry for sale, *paella* on the menu and, in Melilla, a bull ring. Morocco periodically asks for the return of the territory, ironically a mirror image of Spain's claims on Gibraltar across the way. Tensions are well under control.

Unlike mosaics of tiny squares, *zelliges* are enamelled terracotta tiles cut into various geometrical shapes and set into plaster.

Imperial Heart

In the strategic central area of Morocco, two imperial capitals within 60 km (less than 40 miles) of each other but hundreds of years apart vie for sumptuous extremes. Excursions into the surrounding region unearth the glory that was Rome and the mystique of an Islamic saint. To the south, the Middle Atlas hints at the dizzying mountain experience that awaits.

Meknès

The Alaouite Sultan Moulay Ismaïl, who ruled from 1672 to 1727, has been called the Louis XIV of Morocco. If that means thinking big in the pursuit of glory, it's easy to see the link between the two contemporaries. For Louis, Versailles was the ultimate extravagance. For the ruthless Moulay Ismaïl, you don't have to look any further than his capital of Meknès, full of grandiose projects begun during his reign. Some are in ruins, but enough have been preserved to testify to a magnificent dream. Starting with a gateway of remarkable power and beauty.

Bab Mansour

The city walls of Meknès stretch for perhaps 25 km (15 miles), interspersed with gates that are ceremonial or fortress-style or utilitarian. The most wondrous of all is the monumental Bab Mansour, named after the architect, a Christian slave converted to Islam. The symmetry of the enormous ensemble warms the spirit. Take the time to absorb the intricacies of the decorations above the main horseshoe arch and the smaller side arches for the bastions. (Among the inscriptions in graceful calligraphy is mighty praise for Moulay Ismaïl and his son, Moulay Abdallah, who finished the job.)

Mausoleum

Moulay Ismaïl enlisted everybody available to build his city — artisans, labourers, tribesmen and slaves. In his relentless and comprehensive construction programme, he didn't forget to build his own last resting place. Pilgrims, especially country folk, still come to the lavish mausoleum to pray in the memorial mosque. The unpredictable sultan was reputed to have crowds of victims on his conscience, but because of his religious fervour he is still seen as saintly. Non-Muslims are permitted to peer into, but not quite set foot in, the mosque of the Moulay Ismaïl Mausoleum.

Dar Jamaï

A highlight of the medina, Dar Jamaï is a 19th-century palace now serving as a museum of Moroccan arts. A minister of the sultan's court lived in this palace in an enviable state of luxury. Among the works of art and handicrafts on display are carpets from the Middle Atlas mountains, household furnishings, embroidery, decorative wall tiles, pottery and jewellery. The palace itself remains a delight to the eye.

The Souks
Just around the corner from the museum-palace begin the souks, where artisans produce everything from carpet slippers to saddles, from wedding gowns to tea pots. You can see a carpet woven, a table sanded, a fancy kaftan sewn. All the fragrances of the orient are here, from the saffron on sale in giant sacks to the skewered meat sizzling on the grill. Here, too, you can purchase herbs and health foods, including plump, live lizards whose blood is said to be a reliable tonic.

Bou Inania Medersa
This 14th-century religious college surrounds a tiled courtyard equipped with a tinkling marble fountain for meditative background music. It was built about the same time as a medersa of the same name in Fez. Outstanding here is the woodwork—the complex carving of cedar screens enclosing the dormitory.

You can visit the student cells, then climb to the roof for a view of the Grand Mosque next door, with its red-tiled roofs and green-tiled minaret.

Moulay Idris
Pilgrims have climbed the hillsides of this white-walled town north of Meknès for centuries. Here is the tomb of a great-grandson of the Prophet Mohammed, the sultan-saint Moulay Idris, founder of the first Moroccan Arab dynasty. Non-Muslims are forbidden to enter the shrine and adjacent *zaouia,* but the rest of the town is open to infidels, if not necessarily warmly welcoming. The holiest town in the country, Moulay Idris looks inward with a self-sufficient air. You can climb the zigzag streets and look down onto the green tile roofs of the monuments and the countryside of olive trees, pines and cactus.

Volubilis
They came a long way, but the ancient Romans found a majestic site for their farthest-flung African city. The Phoenicians seem to have been here several centuries earlier but by the first century AD this was a key outpost of the Roman province of Mauretania Tingitana. Volubilis looks out on mountains and valleys to inspire a poet—a 360° view of the best of North African scenery. New colonists arriving here at the end of an incredible overland voyage

from the Mediterranean must have been cheered at the familiar sight of cedar trees and a ceremonial arch. Today it's an easy half-day-trip from Meknès, a chance to wander through acres of evocative ruins.

On Site

For a modest admission fee you can follow the path across a negligible ravine and up to the heart of the archaeological site. Few signs inform the visitor, but it's hard to get lost. And should you happen to enter somewhere out of bounds or climb on to delicate stonework a guardian will blow a whistle to restore order.

Among the first sights is a Roman olive oil factory and storage facility. The region is still in the olive business, and the technical side hasn't changed a lot. Nearby, the foundations of the luxurious House of Orpheus show the sophistication of the plumbing and heating; fine mosaics are preserved.

The Forum

At the top of the town, the Forum was the centre of life in Volubilis. Here is the Basilica, with many arches still standing, and the columned Capitol. The Triumphal Arch, incompletely restored but a stately landmark, was dedicated to the Emperor Caracalla. Between the arch and the Tangier

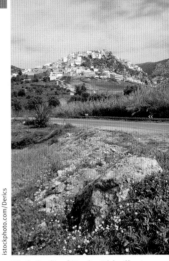
The holy city of Moulay Idris clinging to the hillsides.

Gate runs the main street, Decumanus Maximus, lined by the remains of aristocratic houses and palaces. Some classic mosaics remain where they were unearthed, but many valuable artefacts and statues wound up in museums or farther afield.

Fez

Famous for their self-assurance and sophistication, the people of Fez don't hide their pride in their lively and colourful city, which has been a political, spiritual, intellectual and commercial cen-

Three great museums. Highlights from Roman Morocco are assembled at the **Archaeological Museum** in Rabat, noted for two exquisite bronze busts from Volubilis. Some Volubilis mosaics turn up at **Dar el Makhzen,** the Museum of Moroccan Arts in Tangier, also featuring masterpieces of folk art. In Fez, a 19th-century palace, **Dar Batha,** is now a showplace for Moroccan arts and crafts ranging from calligraphy to carpets.

Huber/Ripani

tre for centuries. Fez can be a jolt for outsiders, mixing the most memorable contrasts: splendours of classical art, the down-to-earth bustle of everyday life, and the stench of medieval industry.

Fez traces its history to the era of Moulay Idris, the 8th century "patron saint". His son, Idris II, continued the work, building a royal palace, a market and town walls, and welcoming talented immigrants from Andalusia. Devout refugees from a Berber pogrom in Kairouan (Tunisia) founded the Karaouine Mosque. This 9th-century institution included what is now the world's oldest existing university (Europe's oldest university, at Bologna, wasn't established until the 11th century). Later dynasties embellished old Fez with fortifications, schools, mosques and shrines. Morocco's first imperial city, Fez stood unchallenged astride the trade routes linking the Sahara and the Mediterranean.

Fes el Bali

The oldest part of Fez, very much a lived-in part of the city, is overpoweringly exotic. You'll want to see Fes el Bali's formal historical monuments, but what will linger longest in your memory is the experience of mingling with ordinary people going about their business in a timeless swirl of outlandish sights and smells. Donkeys are the taxis of the medina, but there are traffic jams in the narrow lanes, and it gets messy underfoot. (Listen for the cry *"balek!",* warning that traffic is directly behind you.) Each craft congregates in its own mini-neighbourhood—tailors squatting in adjacent open shop-fronts, their needles flashing as they stitch a metre a minute; nearby the fragrance of cedar shavings advertises the realm of the carpenters. In the closed world of the medina, the sawdust doesn't go to waste—it fuels the fire that heats the water in the nearby *hammam,* the communal baths.

Bab Bou Jeloud

The most beautiful way in to the medina is through a celebrated gate, Bab Bou Jeloud. Although the style of the decorations is classic "Mauresque", the gate dates from the beginning of the 20th century. Glazed tiles in the most intricate patterns decorate the upper part. Below is a ceremonial portal fit for a sultan on camelback, flanked by smaller, thinner horseshoe-arched gates for pedestrians.

Bou Inania Medersa

Workmanship from the 14th century Merenid dynasty makes the Bou Inania Medersa of Fez one of the country's outstanding monuments. The religious school is divided from a prayer room by a refreshing stream of water channelled into the marble paving of the courtyard. Some splendid wood-carving surrounds the courtyard, and there are more

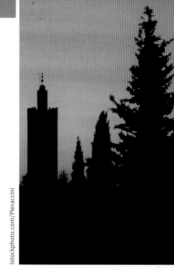

istockphoto.com/Pieraccini

Minarets of Fez in the golden hour.

decorative delights in ceramic tile and stucco.

Just across the street a remarkable medieval clock, no longer in working order, was designed to be the definitive judge of prayer times.

Dar Batha Museum

A spacious garden, home base for a squadron of twittering birds, adds to the appeal of the 19th-century Dar Batha palace, now the setting for a museum of Moroccan arts and crafts. The exhibits range from 14th-century keys, locks and doors to Middle

The ancient stone dyeing vats are still in use in the souk—the colours are a feast for the eye.

hemis.fr/Franck

Atlas carpets so sumptuous that visitors would be crawling over them if they weren't hanging on the walls.

Notices in Arabic and French identify and explain traditional musical instruments, costumes, copper- and brass-work, 16th-century ceramics, ancient books and manuscripts.

Karaouine Mosque

Until the construction of the Hassan II Mosque in Casablanca, the Karaouine Mosque of Fez was the biggest religious structure in Morocco. Founded in the 9th century and expanded in the 10th and 12th centuries, it is surrounded on all sides by the throbbing medina. If you walk in a great circle you will eventually pass each of its 14 doors, each giving the most partial view, but you'll never manage to see all of it. Inside is a 16-aisle prayer hall large enough for 20,000 of the faithful.

Moulay Idris Zaouia

You might suddenly think you were in a church, but the candles and incense on sale just outside the door of the *zaouia* of Moulay Idris are part of a distinctive Islamic cult. Moulay Idris II, who made Fez a great 9th-century city, is buried here. You can see into the edge of the sanctuary, where women pass offerings through a hatch to the tomb of the sultan, considered a saint. This is as close as non-Muslims can get to the blessings thought to be available here.

Fes el Djedid

Fes el Djedid means "Fez the New", but the district is not to be confused with the Ville Nouvelle (New Town) of the French era. Fes el Djedid dates from the 13th century, when the Merenid sultan built a walled precinct of gardens, palaces, forts and, oddly, the Mellah, the Jewish ghetto.

Ville Nouvelle

Divided by broad avenues, this is the centre of commerce, and here the populace congregates for the early evening promenade, punctuated by mint tea at the outdoor cafés.

Tanners and dyers. The most fragrant place to be in the Fez medina is the spice market, where the aromas of mint, saffron and other scents compete for your pleasure. Less alluring is the smell of cloth drying in the dyers' souk. Worst of all is the heavy stench pervading the tanneries, where fresh animal hides are cleaned and shaped, then tanned and dried in hellish heat. The process has hardly changed since the Middle Ages.

You can find anything and everything on place Djemaa el Fna, even couscous made to measure.

Marrakesh

Founded over a thousand years ago, Marrakesh served as capital several times and inherited from those bygone days an unequalled elegance.

The walls of the medina, built in the 12th century, earned it the name of "red city". The high crenellated wall measures 19 km (12 miles) in perimeter, dotted with 200 towers and pierced by over a dozen gateways. You can tour around them in a horse-drawn calèche, discovering along the way some of the highlights of the Almoravid and Almohad dynasties: here the great Bab Doukkala, further on Bab Agnaou, opening onto the kasbah.

With the huge and lively square, Djemaa el Fna, at its heart, the medina is a tangle of narrow, dark alleys, often leading nowhere, and impenetrable living quarters huddled around their respective mosques. In contrast, the New Town to the west, designed during the French Protectorate, has straight, elegant boulevards shaded by palms, olive and orange trees.

The Djemaa el Fna Area

The high-toned historical monuments can come later. First, get a taste of contemporary life in North Africa's most colourful marketplace. With the souks to the north and the kasbah to the south, it is the very soul of the city; as the day wears on, it gets more and more crowded. The name, Assembly of the Dead, comes from the fact that executions were held here in public until the 19th century; chopped-off heads were displayed for all to see.

Djemaa el Fna

At dawn, sellers of freshly pressed orange juice and dates set up their colourful stands in neat rows at one end of the square. The traffic starts rolling — bicycles, scooters, motorbikes, the first horse-drawn carriages, while gradually, the other tradesmen take up their pitch: fortune-tellers and shoe-shine boys sheltering from the sun beneath brightly coloured parasols, women with their henna kits ready to give you a non-permanent tattoo, small boys with bathroom scales to tell your weight. Near the Quessabine mosque, wily herbalists display their magic potions for restoring health and youth, remedies and panaceas; dried plants, ostrich eggs, live iguanas and coloured powders, musk, henna, black soap and Spanish fly.

At lunch time, the tables fill up in the restaurants and cafés along the esplanade: mint tea and ice cream on the ground floor, lunch upstairs on the terrace with a view over the square. There's none better than the Café Glacier and minstrels. Everything is here; you can shop, eat, hire a scribe, have your hair cut or a tooth pulled. It's a dream of an open-air show, and although the tourists love it they make up only a small minority of the crowds, for this is where all of Marrakesh converges—day and night. Mind the pickpockets.

Koutoubia Mosque

Marrakesh is flat, conducive to seeing the sights by bicycle or calèche, horse and carriage. It's so flat that from almost anywhere in town you can see the landmark minaret of the Koutoubia Mosque, 77 m (252 ft) high. It was built from 1184 to 1189, and served as model for the famous Giralda in Seville and the Hassan Tower in Rabat. For its construction, the Almohad king Abd el Moumen chose the site of the former palace of Ali, the last of the Almoravids—it was razed to mark the change of power. The first mosque was also destroyed and rebuilt a few decades later because apparently it was not set precisely in the direction of Mecca. Its name (from *kutubiyin*, manuscript-sellers) is a reference to the booksellers' souk in the same neighbourhood. It has also been called the Golden Apple mosque because of the gilded domes topping the minaret. According to legend, these were

on the south side, where everyone meets up at sunset. That's the busiest time on the square, when trestle tables and barbecues are set up and the air soon fills with smoke carrying enticing smells of grilled meat and spicy lamb sausages. Above the din sound the wailing flutes of the snake charmers, always ready to lift the lid on their cobras and sand vipers when you give them a coin; a few steps away, *gnaoua* musicians (descendants of slaves) dance in their blue costumes. The circus never stops: acrobats, jugglers, story-tellers, fire-eaters, whirling dervishes, musicians made from the melted-down jewels of the wife of sultan Yakoub el Mansour, as penitence for breaking the Ramadan fast.

At the foot of the building spreads a garden shaded by tall palm trees; in the evenings, the townsfolk stroll around in groups with family or friends. Non-Muslims are not permitted to enter the mosque.

La Mamounia
To the west, Avenue Houmman el-Fetouaki sweeps up to Bab el Jedid, one of the busiest gateways into the medina. With beautiful grounds bound on two sides by the city walls, the famous hotel La Mamounia is a fine example of Art Deco architecture. You'll have seen its restaurant in the Hitchcock film, *The Man Who Knew Too Much* (1955). On one side, the rooms look out onto the Koutoubia, on another the peaceful shady gardens, tended by 34 gardeners and full of swooping swallows.

Handicraft Centre
Some 300 m west of the Koutoubia along Avenue Mohammed V, this shopping mall groups a number of boutiques and cooperatives selling handicrafts at fixed prices. There is much less choice than in the souks, but it's a good idea to look in here to get an idea of prices before you venture further.

The Souks and North of the Medina
North of Djemaa el Fna is the most popular sector of the medina, famed for its labyrinthine souks. Beyond, you will find some of the finest and oldest religious monuments of the city, and you will catch a glimpse of typical neighbourhood life.

The Souks
They begin at the very edge of Djemaa el Fna. Spreading in a maze of alleys protected from the sun by makeshift lattices, they stretch north as far as the Ben Youssef mosque. As is the custom, each of the 40 listed corporations has its own little district, so you don't have to go far to compare the prices of a kaftan or a carpet: dried fruit sellers are grouped together in the Kchacha souk, potters in the Fekharine souk, fabric sellers in Smarine, babouche-makers in Smata, metalworkers in Attarine, blacksmiths in Haddadine, leather craftsmen in the renowned Cherratine, while the dyers suspend coloured swatches of wool on reed screens in the Sebbagine souk, further west. It's impossible *not* to get lost—but after all, one of the real pleasures of the souks is wandering around trying to find your way out!

In all, there are over 10,000 people working here (each little shop is generally handed down from father to son). You'll probably have more contact with the middle-men who stock their wares. All manner of necessities and trifles are on sale in the sprawl of covered streets and alleys—pottery, leather ware, wrought iron, clothing, cosmetics and the most bizarre "health foods". Among the sandal-makers you'll discover that those soft-leather pointed slippers *(babouches)* are made with the heel already tucked in. They are designed to slip on and off, as when visiting a mosque. When important transactions take place, bargaining can carry on for hours, fuelled by glasses of mint tea.

On Place Bab Fteuh, just north of Djemaa el Fna, a few merchants have set up shop in former caravanserais. In front of them, basketsellers have taken over the old grain and slave market on Place Rahba Kedima, whose west and south sides are occupied by apothecary's shops with mysterious jars lined up on the shelves, baskets full of dried leaves and herbs, alum stones and a thousand and one remedies. The carpet sellers spread out their wares on the north side of the square.

Ben Youssef Mosque

With a minaret 40 m (131 ft) high, the mosque was founded in the 12th century and modified several times since then, most notably in the 16th century. It is covered by an attractive green-tiled roof. Access to the mosque is prohibited to non-Muslims.

Koubba el-Ba'adiyn

Opposite the entrance to the Ben Youssef Mosque, this splendid early 12th-century building (a public bath) is the oldest in the town and the last surviving example of Almoravid art in Marrakesh. It was long half-buried and excavated only in 1948, revealing a basin for ablutions covered by a splendid dome decorated with floral arabesques intermingled with epigraphic and geometric motifs. An inscription attributes it to the Almoravid king Ali ben Youssef, a great builder, who wanted to adorn the town with grand monuments suited to its rank of capital of North Africa and Andalusia. The koubba was part of the Mosque of Ali, which also included a fountain, a library, a cistern, a hammam and latrines.

Museum of Marrakesh

Housed in the Dar Mnebhi, a palace built at the end of the 19th century for Sultan Abdelaziz's Defence Minister, this private museum, with its gurgling interior fountains, comfortable seats and cosy little café, seems a little out of time and place in the historic heart of the medina. It is devoted exclusively to temporary exhibitions. Works of modern art are displayed on the walls of the old hammams and the kitchens, while more traditional artworks are exhibited in the patios and lounges. Concerts, plays and other shows are performed here too.

Ben Youssef Medersa

In the centre of the medieval medina, this religious school was founded in the 14th century and ornately refurbished from 1563 to 1565 during the reign of the Saadian sultan Abdella Al Ghalib, who made it the largest in the country and decorated it with a profusion of Carrara marble, cedar wood, *zelliges* (coloured mosaics in different shapes) and stucco. It is built on a square plan around a courtyard with a fountain that was used for ablutions. On the east side is a prayer hall with a *mihrab* (niche indicating the direction of Mecca) with particularly fine stucco work in floral, geometric and calligraphic design.

You can go upstairs and visit what were the students' rooms, varying from the most monkish cells to rather grand rooms with a view, with wooden balconies overlooking small courtyards. (For reasons of fair play the room assignments were rotated every Friday.)

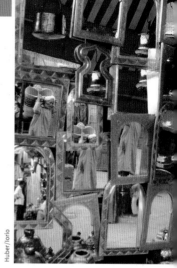

Huber/Iorio

Mirrors capture the everyday life of the souk.

Dar Bellarj

Next to the entrance to the medersa, the "House of Storks", an old hospital where wounded birds were once tended, is now the headquarters of the Moroccan Foundation for Culture. Temporary exhibitions are held in the rooms surrounding the pretty central patio, and you can follow courses in local handicrafts.

Tanners' District

As far as anyone can remember, the Tanners' District has always stretched out around Bab ed Debbah street and the gate of the same name. Today there are still over a dozen workshops here, all of them taking the form of "fields" of basins where the skins are left to soak. Some are dug out of the ground, others are built of stone. The overruling smell is fetid—and the sprigs of mint the guides will give you to waft beneath your nose are not very effective. Four soaks and a number of beatings are required to obtain the best skins: the first, in quicklime, gets rid of the hairs. The next one, mixed with pigeon droppings, makes the leather more supple. The third, in bran, blanches it. The next, mixed with oak bark, gives the leather its brown colour. Then comes the dye bath, sheltered from the sun to stop the colours changing. Most of the tanneries also dye wool, which you can see drying on the rooftops next to the skins.

Sidi Bel Abbès District

Visitors rarely wander through the Sidi Bel Abbès district in the north part of the medina. It is built around the mosque of the same name, dating from the 17th century and difficult to discern above the maze of alleys and covered passageways surrounding it. Venture here for a glimpse of authentic neighbourhood life, with its hidden corners and tiny shops.

On the way, in Amesfah street, look out for the town's most beautiful public fountain, Chrob ou Chouf, against a pink wall and sheltered by a finely carved cedarwood roof. Its name means "Drink and admire" (it is a UNESCO Cultural Heritage site).

Dar el Glaoui

West of the souks, the splendid Glaoui Palace, also known as the Riad Tarifa, is discreetly hidden behind high blank walls. Built at the end of the 19th century for the powerful ruler El Glaoui, it is now home to the services of the town's cultural affairs. The entrance, signalled by a simple red flag, is on Bab Doukkala street, near the crossing with Dar el Glaoui street. Passing through a series of corridors and tiled rooms, you come out into a vast patio planted with orange trees around a little fountain. The east and west wings are in typical Arabic style. To the north and south, the Corinthian pilasters and patterns in cedar wood show western influences.

Bab Doukkala

To the west, Bab Doukkala street leads to the mosque, then to the big gate of the same name. Between them, sheltered from the sun by a latticed roof, is a colourful and popular little market, with fruit and vegetable stalls, date-sellers balancing baskets on their bicycles, butchers' stalls and other overburdened carts.

The Kasbah and Palaces

South of the medina, the kasbah stretches around the Royal Palace, one of the favourite residences of King Hassan II. His son Mohammed VI has given his own preference to another palace further west, near Bab Agnaou. The kasbah opens to the north on the Place des Ferblantiers and in the east blends into the mellah, the old Jewish quarter. Further north, from Djemaa el Fna, you can reach several other palaces.

Riad Zitoun District

South of Djemaa el Fna, this is one of the most picturesque districts of the medina, stretching around two narrow streets reserved for pedestrians and motor scooters, Riad Zitoun el Kedim (the old) and Riad Zitoun el Jedid (the new). To either side spreads an intricate network of alleys and lanes, lined with ancient houses with wooden doors, their walls warm-hued, their windows hidden by grids of wrought-iron, holding their secrets within. There are also several riads—splendid traditional houses—their rooms looking onto a central courtyard, several of which have been transformed into museums or hotels.

Dar Si Saïd

On one side of an alley near Riad Zitoun el Jedid, this cool, late-19th-century palace, one of the most beautiful in the town, houses a museum devoted to Moroccan traditional arts. It was built for Si Saïd Moussa, minister at the time when his brother Ba Ahmed, who resided in the nearby Bahia Palace, was the grand vizir. Several exhibition halls with carved and painted ceilings of cedar wood are set around a pretty tree-shaded patio. The most beautiful rooms, decorated with a profusion of tiles and stucco, are located upstairs: the lofty reception room has a splendid cedarwood ceiling 13 m (43

The Seven Saints. In and around the medina, you will no doubt see the *zaouïas*, or shrines, sheltering the tombs of the Seven Saints of Marrakesh, holy men born between the 12th and 16th centuries. In the 17th century, Sultan Moulay Ismaël inaugurated a pilgrimage which is still followed fervently today, with the pilgrims praying beside one tomb per day. The week-long circuit always begins on a Tuesday at the tomb of Sidi Youssef ben Ali, which is outside the walls southeast of the medina. It ends on the following Monday at that of Sidi Souhaili.

ft) from the ground. In the adjoining room, you can see the alcoves in which the musicians would play, but also the closed balconies with lattices through which the ladies of the household could watch festivities without being seen.

The museum displays a collection of Moroccan Arts. Specialities are Berber artefacts, ancient and modern, from the south of the country—jewellery, costumes, pottery, carpets, furniture, toys and weapons. There is also an important exhibition devoted to woodworking and carving in Morocco, with a fine collection of windows, monumental doors, ornamental grids, carved corbels and lintels, musical instruments and furniture.

Dar Tiskiwin

Located in one of the two alleys leading to Dar Si Saïd, the Dar Tiskiwin Museum is housed in a handsome century-old residence transformed to hold the collections of a Dutch ethnologist who settled down here. There is an interesting permanent exhibition documenting the art of personal adornment in the Sahara, presented in the form of a journey from Morocco to Timbuktu and back again. The collections of jewellery, costumes, carpets and other decorative objects are scattered around the small rooms of the house, around two courtyards, one of which has splendid stucco and cedarwood ornamentation.

El Bahia Palace

An ensemble of houses and annexes all linked together, this palace is quite complicated to navigate, with its succession of courtyards, gardens and reception rooms, mosque, hammam, stables and kitchen garden. A cen-

Storks. Every year, at the end of November, the storks return to Marrakesh. Mostly from Alsace, they spend the winter season in Morocco and nest there before returning northwards at the beginning of summer. Here, it's said that they all leave on July 17. Not at all timid, they set up house on abandoned buildings: you can see them on some of the tours and gateways of the ramparts (Bab Agnaou) and the ruins of El-Badi palace. At the height of the season, there are dozens of them, clacking away and strengthening their nests with branches.

Claude Hervé-Bazin

tury old, it was the residence of the grand vizier Ba Ahmed, who became regent from 1894 to 1900. He took over his father's house (Dar Si-Moussa) and a group of neighbouring homes which he bought after acceding to power. The palace, renowned for the painted wooden ceilings, doors and windows, covers a total area of 8 hectares! Morocco's best craftsmen worked relentlessly for six years, splashing ornamentation in traditional designs everywhere in a carefree spare-no-expense style. Guides gleefully point out the living quarters of the grand vizir's four wives and countless concubines in the harem section, where, for security reasons, only blind musicians entertained and eunuchs served the tea. All the rooms are on the ground floor: Ba Ahmed was small and fat and wary of staircases. He received the members of the government in the Council Chamber, opening onto a small riad shaded by big orange trees. From 1912, the French Resident General to Morocco, General Lyautey, made it his official residence.

Place Ozadria

Also called Place des Ferblantiers, this little square is closed on all sides and is well worth investigating. All the craftsmen working in metal have their workshops here producing lamps, mirrors, wrought iron and tinplate cooking utensils.

El Badi Palace

The legendary king Ahmed el Mansour, the most famous of the Saadians, conqueror of Timbuktu and named "The Golden" so huge was his fortune, built this palace in the 16th century. It once spread over 8 hectares, up to the Kasbah mosque, and comprised 360 rooms—one for each of his four wives and the rest for his concubines. The construction, begun after the Victory of the Three Kings over the Portuguese in 1578, took 25 years to complete. But when the Alaouite dynasty came to power in the 17th century, they ordered destruction of the building. Most of its rich trappings were sent to the new capital, Meknes.

Only the royal reception room has been restored: plans are underway to use it for a Museum of Islamic Art. Among the ruins, you can see the remains of the hammam and the prison. The cells were reserved for political prisoners who never saw the light of day. From the roof terrace, you get a good view over the site, the kasbah and part of the medina.

A splendid 12th-century *minbar*, hailed as one of the greatest masterpieces of Islamic art, can be seen in a small room at the

Outside the studded doors of El Mansour Mosque.

hemis.fr/Du Boisberranger

back of the palace. It was commissioned from craftsmen in Cordoba, Andalusia, by the Almoravid sultan Ali ben Youssef, and took eight long years to complete. It was transported to Marrakesh in pieces, set up in the Mosque of Ali, then transferred to the Koutoubia when the Almohads took over from the Almoravids. After eight centuries, it was removed from the mosque and sent to its present home in the El Badi palace in 1962. With its Kufic inscriptions of verses from the Koran, and finely crafted marquetry panels, it was already hailed as a work of perfection back in the 14th century.

The annual Marrakesh National Festival of Popular Arts is held in the palace between June and August, and it is also home to the International Film Festival in autumn.

The Royal Palace

Walking eastwards from the El Badi palace, you reach the main entrance of the Dar el Makhzen, the only part of the royal palace that is open to the public. Founded in the 12th century, it was expanded in the 16th by the Saadians and then modified again by the Alaouites. On some occasions it's possible to visit the Grand Méchouar (assembly square) near the red gate, Bab Ahmer.

El Mansour Mosque

Also called the Kasbah Mosque, it was built in the late 12th century during the reign of Yacoub el Mansour, the king who went down in history for his victories over the Christians of Spain. However, it was damaged by an explosion in 1574 and had to be rebuilt. Only Muslims can go inside; the interior is decorated with splendid painted wooden ceilings, and the ivory-incrusted *minbar* dates from the 13th century.

Saadian Tombs

Next to the Kasbah Mosque, an alley opens onto the entrance of the tombs of the Saadian princes, at the end of a narrow, winding passageway. The elegant 16th-century burial place of the rulers of the Saadian dynasty was forgotten until the 20th century. Sultan Moulay Ismaïl, who spared no effort to efface the memory of his predecessors, had it walled up. Exquisitely carved Carrara marble is used unsparingly; in those days Moroccan sugar was traded for an equal weight of the finest imported marble.

Under vaulted ceilings reminiscent of Andalusian palaces, the most handsome architectural detail is the *mihrab* (prayer niche) in the first mausoleum you see. Indoors and out, here are the tombs of sultans, princes, officials and servants, all with finely

Four beautiful city gates. Some say the vast 18th-century **Bab Mansour** in Meknès is the most magnificent gate in Morocco. A 20th-century competitor is the brightly decorated **Bab Bou Jeloud** in Fez. Also impressive is the massive but delicately decorated 12th-century gate to the **Oudaïa Kasbah** in Rabat. And the oldest gate in Marrakesh, **Bab Agnaou** (below) has lovely designs and Kufic calligraphy carved into local stone.

hemis.fr/Frumm

detailed carvings of flowers, leaves and calligraphy. The most impressive tomb of all belongs to Ahmed el Mansour, the Saadian who took his troops to Timbuktu, assuring the profitable desert trade in gold and slaves.

Bab Agnaou

The most beautiful of Marrakesh's gateways, Bab Agnaou also dates from the reign of Yakoub el Mansour (12th century). Built in Guéliz sandstone, extracted from the quarry on the outskirts of town, it glows like gold in the setting sun. A great number of storks have taken up residence here, building their nests on the top of the wall.

The Merinid sultan Abou Thabit had the heads of 600 insurgents displayed on neighbouring Bab er Robb in 1308.

The New Town and Gardens

West of the medina, the New Town, created during the French Protectorate, comprises the administrative district of Guéliz (a corruption of the French *église*, church) to the north and the residential district of the Hivernage, to the south. Always boisterous and lively, Guéliz spreads around Avenue Mohammed V, a commercial thoroughfare running towards the ramparts and the Koutoubia. Here and in neighbouring streets, hotels, shopping centres and administrative buildings reveal the smart side of the city. The district ends at Moumen ben Ali Square in the northwest, a crossroads encircled by cafés.

South of Avenue Hassan II and Place de la Liberté, the Hivernage is a peaceful area, its buildings painted a uniform pink and its wide, airy streets lined with orange and jacaranda trees. Today, this former consular district is full of opulent residences, grand hotels and important public buildings such as the Opera, the stadium and Congress Centre.

Markets

North of Avenue Mohammed V, between Rue de la Liberté and Rue Souria is a large covered market. There are many fruit and vegetable stalls, but also souvenir stands where a few craftsmen demonstrate their skills.

To the northeast, between the bus station and the Majorelle Garden, the wholesale market is more or less reserved for the Marrakesh dealers, but many more humble people also set up stands to sell oranges, apples, pumpkins or carrots.

Menara Garden

West of the Hivernage, the Menara Garden is as big as a plantation. Every weekend, families come here to picnic beneath the rows of olive trees. A huge pool in the centre, 2.50 m (8 ft) deep, was created by the first of the Almohad kings in the 12th century; he wanted his soldiers to know how to swim before their departure for Andalusia. The pool is fed constantly by pipes coming down from the Ourika valley, 50 km (30 miles) away. A pretty pavilion, built much later (19th century) to enhance the ruling sultan's daily constitutionals, is reflected in the waters like a mirror—a splendid sight at dusk when the peaks of the Atlas can be discerned beyond it on the horizon. In the evenings, a well-orchestrated display of dance, music, theatre, fountains, fire and fireworks entitled *Al Ménara, Reflets et Merveilles*, is staged here on the pool, with 50 actors and magical images projected onto screens of water: performances at 7 p.m from December to March and at 10 p.m. from April to November. There is also a restaurant, the Café Maure, where you can watch the shows from the shelter of a Berber tent while enjoying your tajine and honey pancakes.

Just beyond the calm and beauty of the garden is a factory, which, the locals claim, cans Morocco's tastiest olives and purest olive oil.

Majorelle Garden

North of Guéliz, this charming little garden will probably provide some of your best memories of Marrakesh. Designed by the French painter Jacques Majorelle, who set up his studio here in

The elegant pavilion in the Menara Garden. | The intense Majorelle blue, on the walls of the artist's studio in the Majorelle Garden, now a museum of Islamic art.

1924, it is a romantic and very personal interpretation of Morocco: stately palm trees and a profusion of plants brought from the four corners of the world are planted along avenues well equipped with seats where you can sit and admire the enchanting perspectives enhanced by a fountain and sparkling lily ponds. Nothing is left to chance. Wherever you look, the pathways are marked out by the famous Ma-

jorelle blue and scattered with rotund plant pots painted in the same intense blue or a lighter shade, bright green and lemon yellow. The garden was open to the public when the painter was still alive, then fell into oblivion when he died as a result of a car accident in 1962. The property was acquired and restored by a trust created by Yves Saint-Laurent (1936–2008), whose ashes are scattered in the garden where he often found refuge and inspiration.

The artist's studio, its plain blue walls partly hidden by masses of bougainvillaea, has been transformed into the Majorelle Museum displaying Islamic works of art from his private collections. They give an excellent overview of all the facets of Islamic art, with a preference for Moroccan objects—jewellery and ornaments, luxurious fabrics, weapons, furniture, ceramics and earthenware pottery, gold objects, carved wood.

Agdal Garden

Begun in the 12th century, the Agdal Garden was expanded by the Saadians and now covers some 400 hectares (nearly 1000 acres). Hidden from sight within walls are citrus and olive groves, irrigated by a complex of channels that originate as far away as the Atlas mountains. The lake-sized pool at the centre of the irrigation system was used for royal boating excursions. Nowadays, considerations of hygiene rule out swimming. On Fridays and some Sundays, when the garden is open to the public, the townsfolk come here to picnic beneath the trees.

Excursions

Thanks to its strategic position at the gateway to the Great South, Marrakesh is an ideal base for excursions to the Atlantic shores or the snowy peaks of the Atlas.

The Palm Grove

Tour operators and taxis offer round trips of some 20 km (12 miles) to explore the remains of the immense *palmeraie* that once spread over the northwest outskirts of town along the road to Casablanca. It was first planted by Yousouf Ibn Tashfin, the Almoravid founder of Marrakesh. If many of the 100,000 trees have been cut down to leave space for hotels and golf courses, some parts still remain, with their mudbrick walls and their irrigation channels. The ingenious system of underground pies *(khettara)* was laid in the 12th century when the trees were planted.

Ourika Valley

The Atlas mountains are a favourite summer holiday spot for the inhabitants of Marrakesh, in particular this valley scattered with Berber villages of mudbrick houses. Fields of wheat, orchards and vegetable plots flourish on the banks of the Ourika wadi; the produce is sold in the local souks: Monday at Tnine-l'Ourika, Friday at Djemma Rhmat. From the little town of **Setti Fatma**, you can walk to the Seven Falls and swim in the pool.

Beyond the valley, 77 km (48 miles) from Marrakesh, is the mountain resort of **Oukaïmeden** (the highest in Africa), much appreciated for its cool climate in summer and for its ski runs in winter. Located on the slopes of Djebel Toubkal, alt. 4,167 m (13,672 ft), the highest point in Morocco and enclosed in a national park, it can get plenty of snow from mid-December to mid-April. There are prehistoric rock carvings near the resort entrance.

Ouzoud Falls

These falls, 156 km (97 miles) northeast of Marrakesh, are the most famous in Morocco and the highest in North Africa. Formed by the Ouzoud *wadi*, a tributary of the country's main waterway, Oum er-Rbia, they cascade from 110 m (360 ft), forming a sheaf of white plumes against the reddish rock, usually highlighted by a rainbow. They are most impressive at the end of spring.

View of the old town of Essaouira from the walls of the Skala fortress.

hemis.fr/Mattes

Resorts

The best parts of the Atlantic coast south of Casablanca were colonized by the 16th-century Portuguese empire. The result is a mixed bag of ports, forts and villages with a charmingly skewed, foreign aspect. Linking them, the coastal highway offers dramatic vistas and access to an infinity of beaches.

El Jadida

The intrepid ancient Phoenicians were here first. The Portuguese started all over again, called the port Mazagan, fortified it and held it against all foes for two and a half centuries. A spacious beach attracts swarms of Moroccan vacationers in summer.

El Jadida (meaning "New City") has a remarkable Portuguese legacy in the ramparts and houses of the old city. Among the historic buildings inside the citadel are the governor's palace, a hospital, a prison, and a church later consecrated as a mosque. The most evocative place in town is the Cistern, an underground storage site four centuries old, in which 25 powerful pillars support the vaulted roof, reflected in the water on the floor.

Safi

A city of around 300,000 people with fuming smokestacks, storage tanks and a fish-processing industry is not likely to be high on any tourist itinerary. But Safi is a natural refuelling stop if you're driving the coast road between El Jadida and Essaouira. Its harbour, the nearest port to Marrakesh, has been important for a couple of thousand years. All the industrial installations make the port about as inviting as a steel mill in summer, but history has left some worthwhile traces. The medina near the port was fortified by the Portuguese. A 16th-century fortress now houses the **National Museum of Ceramics**, concentrating on the work of local potteries, which still produce distinctive blue glazes.

Essaouira

Until Moroccan independence, Essaouira was named Mogador. Its history goes back to Phoenician and Roman times, but the most visible influence is Portuguese: the Skala fortress is a classic 16th-century bastion recalling swashbuckling days. Some modern history: Orson Welles was lengthily based here filming *Othello*. Nowadays the excitement comes from legions of windsurfers who have spread the word internationally: the conditions along Essaouira's endless sandy beach are perfect (though the water is not clean enough for swimming), and the relaxed old town, with its shops and riads, is a winner, too.

istockphoto.com/Nieuwland

istockphoto.com/Huybrechts

Hans Weber

The Port
Follow the gulls to the hardest-working fishing port you've ever seen, just beyond the fortifications. When the big trawlers come home, bucket brigades toss ashore baskets of fish from the ships' holds, to be laid out in trays and iced. Porters in rainwear and padded hats carry the dripping trays on their heads to waiting trucks. Meanwhile, crews prepare the ships and the nets for the next outing. It never stops. On the edge of the port, tempting fish and sea-food lunches are grilled *al fresco* for hungry locals and tourists, and you can watch the fish auction.

For a panoramic view of all the excitement, climb to the top of the square bastion, the Skala, where you can also read the inscriptions on the collection of cannon from the 18th and early 19th centuries. There's a view of two rugged offshore islets, now a bird sanctuary.

The Medina
A French architect, a captive of the sultan, designed Essaouira's unusual old walled town. His log-

Beside the shipyard in Essaouira harbour, the blue fishing boats await their crew; in Safi clay jars await application of their blue glaze; supremely patient, a merchant awaits his first client.

ical grid plan removes a lot of the mystery from the medina, though you can still get slightly lost in the back alleys. The souvenir shopping is good, and you might stumble on a hidden square where salesmen auction second-hand clothing, radios or junk. The sellers proceed around the square holding out their property for inspection and quoting a price; often several rounds are needed before a buyer is found.

Agadir

More than 500 km (310 miles) southwest of Casablanca, Agadir is the place for sunny escapism: lazing on 10 km (6 miles) of soft, golden sand, riding a camel, windsurfing, parasailing, and deep-sea fishing for a shark or for dinner. The evenings bring difficult choices among the shops, the international restaurants, cafés and clubs. All those assets and a new international airport make Agadir the number one tourist resort in Morocco, the sort of resort where they have a menu printed in your language, no matter where you're from.

All that's missing is history. The clock stopped on leap day, February 29, 1960, when an earthquake more ruinous than its Richter rating destroyed the city. King Mohammed V mobilized the stricken nation: "If destiny desired the destruction of Agadir,"

Argan trees. Along the roadsides near Agadir, you'll see goats up in the trees. As tourists drive past, goatherds proudly point to the agility of their charges. The climbing goats are not nearly so special as the trees, which are argans *(Argania spinosa)*, which grow only in this small area of Morocco. Argans are rich in oil-rich nutty fruit—that's what the gourmet goats are after—and the wood itself makes excellent fuel. The nuts are harvested and processed by Berber women, then pressed for the precious oil used for cooking and cosmetics and now exported worldwide.

he said, "its reconstruction depends on our faith and determination."

The New City

Post-quake Agadir was built on seismically benign flatlands south of the zone of doom. The centre of the new city is a noisy hustle and bustle of concrete, commerce and traffic, but there are pedestrian malls and parks to relieve the urban stress, and an aviary called the Valley of the Birds. Beyond the business centre the city planners laid out industrial and residential zones. They reserved the choicest real estate, paralleling the bay, for the hotel strip. The tourist sector's expansion goes on for miles, with no end in sight. The same could be said for the glorious beach.

The Kasbah

Discreet signs point the way to a winding road up to the top of a great hill where the ruins of the old town and the remains of thousands of earthquake victims lie within the walls of the old kasbah. You can walk or take a taxi from the main city. The reinforced ochre ramparts are essentially all that's left. There's a gripping view out, especially at dusk, from the hilltop overlooking Agadir's port, the new city and the Atlantic. Camels are available for picture-posing and for rides. Inevitably, souvenir vendors hustle here, immune to the melancholy history of the site.

The highly developed, modern port of Agadir is worth a visit (but take your passport). Big-time fish auctions are scheduled twice daily, in the morning and afternoon, and there are good fish restaurants, as well as informal outdoor grills.

Tafraoute

Excursions from Agadir cut through mountain landscapes into the Ameln Valley, or Valley of Almonds, its charming villages and its main town, Tafraoute. The right time to go is February, when the almond orchards are in blossom. Tafraoute itself adjoins a palm grove, with surreal granite outcrops just above, and the Anti-Atlas in the distance.

Taroudant

The red walls encircling Taroudant are big and powerful enough to protect a metropolis, but everything within is low-slung and village-like. There are only two main squares, between which you can get your bearings. A practical means of transport is the *calèche,* a horse-drawn carriage.

Five inviting beaches. From the Mediterranean to the Atlantic, here are some of the best beaches, secluded coves or great sandy expanses. **Al Hoceïma,** "pearl of the Mediterranean", backed by the Rif mountains; **Mohammedia,** a favourite of nearby Casablanca; **El Jadida,** ever-lively Atlantic resort; **Oualidia,** small family resort; **Agadir,** giant, gently sloping, sunny beach.

The crenellated city walls are pierced by five gates. Long before it was fortified, Taroudant was the ancient capital of the fertile Souss plain, with its olive and citrus orchards. After many ups and downs, going back to the 11th century, good times came in the 16th century under the Saadian dynasty, which made Taroudant its capital before choosing Marrakesh. The Alaouite sultan Moulay Ismaïl punished the town in 1687, wiping out most of the citizens and their homes. The walls were restored but Taroudant never reached its earlier prominence again.

The Souks
No great historical or architectural monuments grace Taroudant, but just roaming around the old town is a pleasure. Tourists being far fewer than in Agadir or Marrakesh, the salesmanship is relatively low-key. The local "bargains" include antique jewellery and weapons (antiquity sometimes simulated), stone carvings, carpets, and handicrafts in general. The souks are varied and rich in local colour.

Spring carpets the countryside with colour. | Boxy houses in red and pink stare out at the world from a village near Tafraoute. | A donkey helps with the harvest in the Souss region.

istockphoto.com/Gillet

Michel Teuler

hemis.fr/Gardel

Aït Benhaddou near Ouarzazate, one of Morocco's best-preserved fortified villages.

The South

Morocco's oases are located on the lower foothills of the Atlas Mountains and beyond, at the edge of the Sahara, along a line drawn between Er Rachidia Ouarzazate and Goulimine, to the east and south of Marrakesh.

The most frequently visited are those of Ouarzazate and Zagora in the south, and to a lesser extent those in the region of Erfoud and the Tafilalt in the east. The remoter oases deep in the south near Tata, in Berber territory, offer less spectacular landscapes, but it is still worth making the effort to get there.

Dadès Valley

The 300 km (190 miles) of tarred road leading from Ouarzazate to the Tafilalt, through the Dadès Valley, offer the opportunity to see a series of natural sites which are among the most impressive Morocco has to offer. Confined between the High Atlas and the Anti-Atlas ranges, the Dadès Valley contrasts the most arid scenery and heartlifting oases. Along the way are kasbahs, ksour palm groves and deep gorges.

Aït Benhaddou

Travelling overland from Marrakech to Ouarzazate by the superb **Tizi n'Tichka** pass (altitude over 2,200 m), don't fail to stop at Aït Benhaddou, a few kilometres before Ouarzazate. Listed as a World Heritage site by UNESCO, this fortified village up on the cliffside is one of the best-preserved and most spectacular in the country.

Ouarzazate

The gateway to the desert is an old French garrison town straggling along a wide main street 5 km (3 miles) long. Now Ouarzazate is a Moroccan army town with soldiers on bicycles trundling past the carpet salesmen. Local luxury hotels cater not only to coachloads of tourists anticipating their safaris but also to international film crews. Somewhere in Ouarzazate you're almost bound to bump into a recognizable movie actor or at least a temperamental cameraman. It all started in the 1960s with *Lawrence of Arabia*. The area is so well endowed in sunshine, dunes, camels and low-budget extras that the cameras of several nations have never stopped grinding out their epics here.

Ouarzazate's principal historical monument, at the crest of Avenue Mohammed V, is a kasbah, or feudal family castle. **Kasbah Taorirt** was built by the Glaoui warlords, who ruled by wile and force of arms over much of southern Morocco in the 19th century and well into the 20th. In its heyday the kasbah housed many relatives of the chiefs as well as an army of hangers-on, servants and craftsmen. Guides lead visitors through restored parts of the complex, most enthusiastically the former wives' quarters, recalling anecdotes of life in the harem. The traditional construction techniques, using palm wood, straw and mud, are readily visible.

From the upper storeys there's a view of the modern **El Mansour dam** that provides water and electricity for the district. The lake created by the dam surrounds an island topped by a ruined kasbah, and provides an unexpected opportunity for swimming or rowing in the midst of a desolate red landscape.

Skoura

Skoura's oasis has some remarkable *pisé* buildings against a glorious backdrop formed by the snowy peaks of the Great Atlas. Take care if you wander into the palm grove at the edge of the town; it's easy to lose your way in this labyrinth of vegetation.

Valley of Roses

The fortified village of **El Kelaa des M'Gouna** is renowned for its roses, whose petals are used for making rosewater. A road from here leads to the wonderful Valley of Roses and its pinkish-red cliffs that give it a unique charm. Like the nearby gorges of Dadès and Todra, the valley is a wonderful place for hiking.

Dadès Gorges

Starting at **Boumalne du Dadès**, the road into the grandiose Dadès Gorges cuts through high cliffs of ever more striking colours. When the weather is dry, intrepid travellers reach the gorges by hiking over the Atlas mountains from those of Todra, to the east.

Tinerhir

The town lies on the road from Boumalne to Er Rachidia in the east, at an altitude of more than 1,000 m (3,300 ft). Its palm grove stretches to the foothills of the Atlas mountains. The view is extraordinary, and it's worth spending an hour or two (before the sun gets too hot) observing the daily life of the people at work around the irrigation channels, in the orchards and the fields. This oasis is without question one of the most beautiful and most prosperous in the country.

Todra Gorges

Tinerhir is the gateway to the Todra Gorges. On the way into the mountains, the roadside villages, many in ruins, are as colourful as the majestic cliffs, some towering 300 m (nearly 1,000 ft) high.

Southern Route

Another way to reach the Tafilalt from Ouarzazate is by the old *piste*, now tarred. The road takes you over interminable, monotonous, rocky plateaux, oppressed by a leaden sun, and you're likely to meet more camels than fellow-drivers. For 250 km (160 miles), the only reprieve is provided by the oases of **Tazzarine** and then **Alnif**, known for its fossils and its pleasant shady palm grove.

The Tafilalt

This is Morocco's most important oasis, where a succession of palm groves, cultivated fields and *ksour* stretch more than 100 km (60 miles) from Rissani to Erfoud and north to the crossroads town of Er Rachidia. All around are great outcrops of black rocks crammed with fossils that children sell for a few *dirhams* by the road or at stopover points.

Er Rachidia

It used to be known as Ksar es Souk when it was a French Foreign Legion fort. It is a strategic base for several excursions, and can be pleasant in the evenings when the streets are lively.

Meski

A little to the south of Er Rachidia, the palm grove at Meski is irrigated by the Blue Springs, a natural groundwater pool named for the "Blue Men" of the desert, the Tuareg, for whom Meski was an obligatory halt. (Tuareg men veil their faces day and night—the women never—with a length of indigo-dyed cotton.) Beyond, one *ksar* after another follows the course of the Ziz river until it runs out on the edge of the desert.

Meski still makes a welcome and refreshing stop for those on their way further south.

Erfoud

In the heart of the oasis, Erfoud is an unprepossessing town, except during the October Date Festival.

On the road to Tinerhir, beyond **Jorf**, you'll notice on each side of the road hundreds of little craters, a meter or so high. They are in fact wells, channelling deep beneath the earth to reach ground water collected a great distance away.

Rissani

For centuries Rissani, the capital of the Tafilalt region, was the last flicker of civilization for the southbound caravans. It was here that cargoes of metals, fabrics, dates and especially salt, were loaded onto the camels. Called the cradle of the Alaouite dynasty, this weatherbeaten village is where the ancestors of the present king established their religious power before triumphing in the 17th century.

A trio of sparrows make themselves at home in an old kasbah.

Nowadays, there's scarcely a trace of that prosperous era when more than 100,000 people lived here, spread out in 600 settlements, and it takes a fertile imagination to conjure up an idea of its former glory. However, if you follow the rutted road that loops around Rissani, you will discover sleepy villages with winding lanes of baked-clay dwellings, huddled together in the suffocating heat.

Here the landscape is fairly flat; the desert is on the doorstep. The further you venture, the more the desert encroaches, finally engulfing the last palm trees and receding crops.

Erg Chebbi

You'll need a four-wheel drive vehicle to make the detour to the dunes. Erg Chebbi, near the village of **Merzouga**, is the biggest sand dune in the country. It rises as high as 150 m (nearly 500 ft) and goes on for miles. It's a great place to be at daybreak. Camel rides into the scorching desert can be arranged from here—and once you get used to the loping gait you'll agree it's the best way to go. You can also hike through the sand.

Southern Oases

The road southeastwards from Ouarzazate to Zagora yields sensational scenery: from stony desert across mile-high mountains, into the Drâa Valley with its historic kasbahs and dreamy palm groves. Few people are seen except for goatherd children selling dates in little straw baskets and women enjoying the desert luxury of washing clothes in a stream. The literal high-point of the journey is the **Tizi n'Tinififft** pass, alt. 1,660 m (5,446 ft).

Fint

Scarcely 15 km (9 miles) from Ouarzazate, a detour from the main road, you suddenly emerge from a setting of rocky black hills into a splash of green in the hollow of a gorge. Fint oasis has served as the location for several films, but the inhabitants still follow their old ways. If you venture along the winding paths of the palm grove, you'll discover a friendly, appealing people, living frugally from the fruit of their labour.

Drâa Valley

From Agdz to Mhamid, the two ends of the Drâa Valley, the river runs for 200 km (125 miles), irrigating palm groves and crops before vanishing into the sands of the desert. All along the valley, oleanders, date palms and acacias mingle with the ochre shades of the earth. It is a splendid landscape, whose changing colours are seen at their best during the first and last hours of daylight. A sprinkling of mysterious kasbahs and ksour are set back from the road. The windblown *pisé* walls often have elaborately carved designs. The settlements recall ancient times when the sedentary populations had to battle against plundering bands of nomads from the south, come to help themselves to the riches of this fertile province.

Zagora

A jokey direction sign in the centre of town proclaims that Timbuktu is 52 days away, by camel. As you take the inevitable picture you'll probably be offered the services of so-called false guides, who pester tourists at every opportunity. If you want a "real" guide, your hotel or the tourist office can provide a legitimate, knowledgeable professional— much cheaper than the tricksters. They will also show you the shops where the much sought-after carpets from the Drâa Valley are offered for sale side-by-side with those made by the Tuareg tribes.

On the top of the Zagora mountain, the remains of an Almoravid fortress can still be seen. The road doesn't quite run out in Zagora, but this is where four-wheel drive vehicles come into their own. Here, too, you can arrange excursions by camel. The caravans still navigate by the stars, which seem to shine more brightly here in the desert. Even if you never sink into a dune, your first sunset in Zagora will confirm that the mystique is intact.

Amazraou

The palm groves of Amazraou are a refreshing antidote to the stress of sightseeing. Sip a cool drink or a mint tea and wait for the dates to fall from the trees, or do something strenuous like visiting the old Jewish kasbah. Most of the Jews of Amazraou, who

A compulsory photo stop in Zagora.

made and traded silver jewellery, emigrated in 1958, but the synagogue still stands. Berbers have taken over some of the silver workshops.

Tamegroute

This village is distinguished by a *zaouia*, or religious sanctuary, founded in the 17th century. Its Koranic Library, which may be visited, contains books and manuscripts up to nine centuries old. There are precious books on science and religion dating from Andalusia's golden age and venerable illuminated tracts.

Mhamid

The paved road from Zagora finally runs out after 90 km (55 miles) in Mhamid. On the way, at **Tinfou**, are some small but evocative sand dunes. Amenable camels are available for photography sessions or excursions. Mhamid is the last oasis before the Sahara. It is here that you are most likely to meet up with the Tuareg "Blue Men", who come on market days to exchange carpets and craftware for staples.

Taliouine

Some 100 km (60 miles) east of Taroudant on the road to Ouarzazate, Taliouine makes a good stopover for visitors heading south over the Anti-Atlas into Berber lands. This little village in the Djebel Sirwa area specializes in saffron, culled from the crocus plants growing in the gardens of the oasis. A cooperative on the edge of town sells the golden spice at a reasonable price. It's used in cooking, but also as a colouring and an antispasmodic medicine.

The Far South

The route to Tata and beyond reveals another side to Morocco, allowing contact with places and people which makes it arguably more authentic.

Tata

You have to cross the Anti-Atlas to reach Tata. The road climbs to an altitude of 2,000 m (6,500 ft), through an untamed landscape of sparse vegetation and rocky canyons striped in many colours. Then Tata heaves into view. The principal town of Tata province, with rose-coloured walls and arcaded streets, it has all the commodities a tourist may need. It stands in the middle of a lovely oasis watered by three wadis which rise in the Anti-Atlas. A palm grove and spring offer pleasant respite from the searing heat.

Akka

An old piste, now tarred, links Tata with Goulimine. There's very little traffic on this road, which crosses wide, empty plateaus open to the Sahara for 300 km (more than 185 miles). Whipped by a scorching wind, sand from the desert mingles with the rocks and stones of the Atlas, while here and there the first dunes appear. Now and then you'll meet a flock of goats along the road, indicating the proximity of a village. Akka, with its low-profile houses and sandswept streets, is planted with date palms and various other fruit trees. In the palm grove you'll see the remains of the *mellah,* the old Jewish quarter, on the hillside.

Amtoudi

After Akka you will pass several other oases, all on the old caravan route from the Sahara: Tisgui, Icht and its fortified village, Foum el-Hassan (known for its rock carvings), Tarhjijt, then Tagmoute on the road to Amtoudi, the most famous of all the oases in the region, and the most vis-

ited. An old kasbah surveys it from on high, renowned for its medieval communal granary (Agadir Id Aïssa). Climb up for a stunning view of the gorges carved out in the bed of the wadi, sheltering a wide variety of fruit trees. Close to the palm grove, you can swim in a natural spring.

Goulimine

Tuaregs still gather in Goulimine for the summer *moussem* (festival) and camel market. This last is also held on Saturdays, mainly for the benefit of day trippers. At other times, you may be the only foreigner; you'll feel as if you're light years away from Marrakesh and the coastal resorts.

Monday in Tinzouline. The village of Tinzouline in the Drâa Valley, halfway between Agdz and Zagora, features a lively regional market on Mondays. In season there's a vast trade in dates, packed in standard boxes, which are transferred from grower to wholesaler almost before you know what's happening. An itinerant blacksmith forges shoes for mules brought to the village for the occasion. Sensitive visitors should keep their distance from the working abattoir in the midst of the market.

The shifting sands of Erg Chebbi, near the small town of Merzouga.

Huber/Ripani

OASES AND DESERT

A cool, green island hidden in the heart of the desert, a sanctuary, the paradise of Allah: the very word "oasis" conjures up an image of peace and tranquillity. The desert is ever-changing: rocky here and sandy there, blazing hot by day and cold at night, fearsome on one side, poetic on the other.

Illusion and Reality

Just looking at the way a few splotches of grey scrub struggle to survive may make you feel thirsty—and heighten the delight when you sight an oasis. The camels, of course, are one-humped dromedaries.

The Heyday of the Oases

Their roots go back to ancient times, but it was in the Middle Ages that the Saharan oases knew their days of glory. With the development of trade in Europe, and the establishment of commercial routes between Europe and black Africa, the oasis was not only a vital resting place for the desert caravans but also a supply post where provisions could be loaded. Setting out from Gao or Timbuktu, the seemingly endless caravans numbered thousands of camels laden with salt, and especially gold. These goods enabled the merchants around the western Mediterranean coast to purchase yet more valuable commodities, such as spices from the Orient or even further afield.

At the same time, the oases became important agricultural centres. In order to exploit this lucrative business, huge engineering projects, especially in irrigation, were undertaken in Morocco from the end of the 8th century, under the Merinids. Great wealth passed through the oases of North Africa, and it was not uncommon for an oasis such as the Tafilalt, to the east of Marrakesh, to number up to 100,000 inhabitants living in several hundreds of fortified villages.

The Decline

After the 16th century, the discovery of the New World, and the promise of treasures it held in store, sounded the death-knell for trans-Saharan trade and the great caravans of the nomadic peoples.

Europe was no longer interested in African gold, hitherto so coveted. They preferred American gold, discovered in quantity and outrageously exploited by the Spaniards. The importance and splendour of the Saharan oases began to decline.

Despite the unhappy reality, the wonderful image of a rich patch of greenery in the midst of an adverse environment long remained fixed in the European consciousness. This was the era of the romantic novel, transporting whole generations in their imagination to the golden, sandy wastes. For the better part of a century, from the end of the 19th to the middle of the 20th, the oasis was something of a mirage.

Perhaps even more than the purple prose of popular literature, the lack of knowledge of the Sahara's realities contributed towards sustaining the myth. Until the early 1950s, the desert was scarcely more than a large blank space on the map. Little explored and largely ignored, the desert was left to itself. The general public only became aware of its existence with the discovery of oil. They then began to hear about oases where the populations were often living in conditions of extreme hardship. The disappearance of the caravans and the evolution of society had engendered great changes in the economic and social life of the oases. As in rural areas the world over, many of the young people had left to seek their fortunes in the towns. At the same time, agricultural activity was completely disrupted by the opening of new markets and the appearance of new production methods. The oases opened up to the outside world, with all the consequences that implied.

The Oasis Today

Nowadays, depending on the region, the situation has changed. In Morocco, an agricultural tradition persists: flourishing in the rich palm-groves of Tinerhir at the gateway to the Todra Gorge; much less prosperous in many of the southern oases. But rich or poor, they all have one feature in common: the caravans of yesterday have been replaced by coach-loads of tourists.

What is an Oasis?

The gentle murmur of water bubbling from the spring and flowing along the irrigation canals, the pleasant coolness of gardens where vegetables and cereals grow, the green plumes of majestic palm trees: such is the magic of an oasis. At first glance they may all seem to follow the same pattern; in fact you'll soon learn how to discern their individual character.

From Mountain to Desert

Initially, all oases were formed by a clump of vegetation that sprouted spontaneously. They are strung like beads along dry desert valleys, or encircle the base of arid mountains, wherever underground water comes close to the surface. *Wadis* are intermittent streams that well up only after heavy rain, but they often have a hidden subterranean flow. Some oases can stretch over several tens of miles, like the Tafilalt oasis in the region of Erfoud, or the Drâa Valley, a wadi south of Ouarzazate.

In Morocco, the "mountain oases" are more numerous. They are mostly found on the high plateaux along the foothills of the Atlas, carving gorges and valleys from the red and brown rock. The isolated "desert oases" are mainly scattered in the south and along the Algerian border.

The Source of Life

Whatever their setting, all oases owe their existence to the presence of water. Whether it has collected underground or on the surface, or flows in the wadis rushing down from the mountains, it is essential. The hostile desert environment could not have been exploited without it.

The water is divided into three main categories. Spring and well water is reserved for human consumption; collected in ponds it is used for bathing, washing clothes and for watering livestock; the rest irrigates the crops. Traditionally, large, clay-lined holding basins serve as reservoirs. Main channels, *séguias*, lead from these basins and are further divided into secondary channels called *masraf*, carrying the water out to the smallest cultivated plot. An ingenious underground drainage system, the *khettara*, completes the installation.

Paradoxically, there's no lack of water in the desert. The only difficulty is bringing it to the surface. Already in medieval times, gigantic engineering projects were undertaken in the Moroccan oases to draw up water to irrigate the land. It was then that agricultural production began to develop, eventually transforming the oases into veritable larders.

Lord of the Oasis

Another common feature of all the oases is the palm tree. Of the many crops to be found there, the date palm, *Phoenix dactylifera*, best symbolizes the oasis—with good reason. It flourishes beside patches of ground water or on the river banks, a noble tree with its feet in the water and its head in the sun. It has been cultivated and prized as the staple food and chief source of wealth in the oases since the remotest antiquity.

Hanging from its branches are great clusters of "fingers of light"—*deglet nour,* the golden dates now widely exported and which for generations have provided a highly energetic food for local populations. Over half the weight of the dried fruit is sugar.

Every part of the palm is valuable: the trunk provides timber to build houses; the midribs of the leaves are handy for fencing; the leaves themselves are used for basket-weaving; the leaf bases and fruit stalks are for fuel, and even the date stones are used to feed the camels. Robust, the date palm is highly productive when properly managed, yielding up to 15 tons of dates per hectare per year. Especially in the south, the palm has displaced other less profitable or more delicate crops, transforming ancient gardens into immense palm groves of up to 35,000 trees, as at Tleta Tagmoute near Tata.

In the heart of the most beautiful oases, you will also discover a jungle of vegetation and a profusion of fresh vegetables. Carrots, turnips, lentils, watermelons, tomatoes and other crops grow in rotation all year round, among terraces of olives, figs, almonds, peaches, apricots and other fruit trees. To complete the picture, plantations of wheat, maize and cereals make a pleasing patchwork of colour.

Kasbah and Ksour

The dwellings are generally grouped together in a higher, drier zone, so as not to waste the smallest strip of fertile land and to better protect the crops from human depredation.

The oasis is a fragile environment. The springs dry up after periods of drought; the wells are choked if a sandstorm blows, burying the palms beneath the dunes. In order to shelter from the elements, but mainly to protect themselves against invaders, the local populations reinforced their villages and homes. Their fortified villages are called *ksour* (singular: *ksar*). For further protection, wealthy warlords set up imposing strongholds, *kasbahs*. Built of mud on stone foundations, these are mainly found in the south and along the banks of the Drâa and the Dadès. There is no danger of attack nowadays, but the oasis dwellers continue to live like their ancestors in houses of *pisé*—a combination of clay, stone and straw—with hardly a concession to modernity. When you walk into one of these villages and savour its particular atmosphere, you might easily believe you have stepped back in time.

Surviving the Desert

If you travel independently, then you should take one or two sensi-

ble precautions. Make sure that your vehicle is in good condition. As petrol stations are few and far between, top up the tank whenever you can, even if it is half full. Make sure you have a sufficient supply of water, and remember to drink frequently. Do not set out on a difficult journey without appropriate equipment, and obtain as much information as you can beforehand. Do not drive at night; it is always dangerous—even during daylight it isn't always easy to find the right road.

During the day, drive carefully, watch out for other vehicles, pedestrians and animals, and pay attention to the state of the road. If your vehicle breaks down, stay near it instead of wandering off for help. Make sure the battery of your mobile phone is fully recharged before setting out.

Whether you're driving, travelling by bus or by camel, you must remember to protect yourself adequately from the heat. You will need a hat and sunglasses, a sweater for night time and high altitudes, and stout walking shoes. Your clothes should be lightweight, preferably in pale colours.

Tinerhir, gateway to the Todra Gorges, surrounded by palm groves. | A cluster of golden dates. | Traditional desert transport.

UNDERSTANDING MOROCCO

Art

The Koran proscribes representations of living things, so Islamic art developed in abstract directions. Thus floral, geometric and calligraphic decorations embellish everything from the walls of mosques to ceramic tiles. The intricately intertwined flowers, leaves and geometrical motifs came to be called arabesque designs. The ban on figurative art is not total in Morocco. In art galleries and markets you'll see modern paintings of scenery, animals and even people—and some avant-garde abstractions, too.

Hammam

The institution goes back to the ancient Roman tradition, but it's part of the Islamic requirement of cleanliness. Moroccans enjoy the relaxation of public baths. When they are alongside mosques, hammams are ritual baths, and non-Muslims may not be welcome. Otherwise they are a gathering place, usually scheduled for men early in the morning and women later. The piping hot steam baths are intended to alternate with cold-water relief. A massage and a nap round off the treatment.

Islam

The word literally means "submission", as in "submission to the will of God", or Allah. The youngest of the world's principal religions, Islam is the official state religion of Morocco. At the beginning of the 7th century, the faith's founder, a merchant from Mecca named Mohammed, heard divine instructions and compiled the word of God in the Koran (meaning "recitation"). Before the century was out, the new religion came to Morocco. The present ruler, who traces his ancestry to the Prophet, is the spiritual as well as political leader of the nation.

The Five Pillars of Islam affect every Moroccan's daily life. The creed must be recited: "There is no god but God, and Mohammed is his prophet." Prayers are scheduled five times daily, and communally in the mosque on Friday. A Muslim has to be charitable. During the holy month of Ramadan, strict rules of abstinence and piety must be respected. And everyone able to do so must make a pilgrimage to Mecca (in Saudi Arabia) at least once in a lifetime.

Starting before dawn, the chant of the muezzin calls the

faithful to prayer. In some countries the call is recorded and transmitted by loudspeaker, but in Morocco the voice from the heights of the minaret, even when electronically amplified, is "live". Other religions summon the faithful to services by horns or bells, but Mohammed himself is said to have found the human voice preferable for the purpose.

Languages

The North African version of spoken Arabic is a long way from classical Arabic or the language of, say, Egypt. Colloquial Berber is spoken by a strong minority of the population—in three dialects, depending on the region. French is very widely understood everywhere. In northern Morocco, for historical reasons, Spanish is the principal foreign language. English has growing impact in commercial and tourist circles, and in tourist areas German is ever more widely known.

Moussem

Most of the hundreds of celebrations called *moussem* venerate local saints. Combining religious and social elements, they can be as simple as a glorified market day or as elaborate as a full-scale folklore festival, with music, dancing, feasting and *fantasias*, the spectacular displays of horsemanship. They happen in all parts of the country all the time but the best chance of stumbling on them occurs in August, September and October, when they double as harvest festivals.

Music

You may be reminded of the wail of the Andalusian flamenco, but the music of Morocco is as varied as it is difficult for the outsider to digest. If the harmonies perplex, the rhythms are compelling. The instruments can be flutes, lutes, woodwinds, fiddles and tambourines, the voices sad or exalted. The influences are Berber, Arab, Jewish, Spanish and international. Relax and give it a try.

Ramadan

The lunar calendar determines the dates of religious holidays, while the civic holidays follow the western calendar. Independence Day always falls on November 18, but Ramadan can be any time, depending on the moon's schedule. The holy month requires fasting from sun-up to sunset. Nightfall brings feasting and celebrations that more than compensate for the asceticism.

In the souk you can watch the craftsmen at work.

SHOPPING

For shoppers visiting Morocco, the thrill of the hunt may be as much fun as the prize. In the mysterious, fragrant atmosphere of the souks you finally see what you want. Even if you don't meet the artisan who created the finest souvenir of your trip, you'll remember the shop or stall where you found it, and the charming salesman who convinced you this was just what you needed. Later, if hindsight shows you paid too much, regret nothing—just chalk it up to the entertainment value of the experience.

Where to Shop

In the medina, you can watch the artisans hammering out copper trays, forging original jewellery and sewing kaftans with flashing needles. You can't shop any closer to the source. The trouble is knowing the price. For Moroccans, haggling is a way for buyer and seller to get to know each other and the real value of the product in question. If this game intimidates or bores you, look for an *ensemble artisanal,* a government-sponsored shop featuring a wide variety of quality goods at fixed prices. At these centres you can see what's available, learn the going prices, and, if you're smitten, buy without pressure. Or return to the souks with renewed confidence in the value of things and haggle the day away.

Carpets

Carpet weaving is the very oldest skill in the Moroccan repertory. The output is divided into two main categories: city and country carpets. The centres of production are Rabat, Meknès, Fez and Marrakesh. You may be able to visit a cooperative where nimble-fingered apprentice girls aged 6 or 7 weave the simple borders of rugs to be filled in by experts, following the complex diagrams of staff designers. More spontaneously, countrywomen create highly prized Berber carpets in the Atlas mountains and as far south as the Ouarzazate region. Keep your eyes peeled for carpets hanging out in villages and at weekly markets in off-beat towns. Irregularity in the design or shape is proof of authenticity.

Clothing

It's hard to resist the urge to buy a burnoose or a fez or some other item of Moroccan clothing to show off to friends. At worst they can be useful at costume parties. The best bet is the kaftan, the all-encompassing woman's dress, which comes in luxuriously embroidered varieties—bound to elicit admiring reactions and interesting conversations when you're entertaining at home.

Jewellery

Morocco's Jews were always the specialists in creating and selling jewellery. Most have emigrated now, yet interesting pieces can still be found. Gold is a favourite medium in the cities, silver in the villages and in the mountains. Silver alone or combined with amber turns up in necklaces, heavy brooches and wrist-, arm- and ankle-bracelets. Gold can be the setting for precious stones in rings, necklaces and earrings.

Leather Goods

The leather of Morocco is so celebrated that the English language has linked the country and the product since at least the 17th century. Precious books are morocco bound. The French were similarly impressed when they began to use the word *maroquinerie* to mean leather goods in general. The softest leather is used for everything from purses and desk sets to those comfortable Arabian-nights slippers called *babouches*. You'll also be offered leather luggage, wallets, belts, cushions and saddles. Fez and Marrakesh have the principal traditional tanneries.

Metalwork

You'll hear them before you see them—artisans chipping away, decorating copper and brass plates, bowls or ashtrays, with geometric designs, swirls and arabesques. Wrought-iron experts produce kasbah-style lamps, grills, mirror frames and candlesticks. Or you can take home a tea-pot of silver or pewter to keep alive the memory of mint tea.

Stones

In Taroudant the local limestone is worked into elaborately decorated candlesticks, boxes and paperweights. Along mountain roads, local children and more forceful adults reflect the sun into your eyes from rough pieces of quartz, amethyst and crystal they are selling. Prices vary greatly.

Wickerwork

There's no end to the choice of wickerwork on sale all around the country—baskets, mats, boxes, sun hats. The biggest variety is sold in the souks of Tetouan, Salé, Fez and Marrakesh.

Woodwork

Aromatic cedar takes on a variety of forms, from chairs and inlaid boxes to figurines and chess sets. In Essaouira they are famous for working thuya, a multicoloured hardwood that comes to a high gloss and retains its fragrance. In Fez and Tetouan you will find painted chests, boxes of all sizes and cradles.

Market Days

Some of the most animated weekly markets, at which tradesmen, artisans and country folk converge colourfully:

Agadir:	Saturday, Sunday
Chaouen:	Thursday
Goulimine:	Saturday (camel market)
Marrakesh:	Thursday (camel market)
Ouarzazate:	Sunday
Rissani:	Sunday, Tuesday and Thursday
Taroudant:	Friday
Tiznit:	Thursday and Friday
Zagora:	Wednesday and Thursday

The carpet patterns may be irregular; that is part of their charm. | Traditional brass lamps can be adapted for candles or electric bulbs. | A plate design begins to take shape. | Herbs and spices (and while you're there, stock up on argan oil).

Author's Image

istockphoto.com/Randall

Fotolia.com/Jakezc

istockphoto.com/Mazurek

Almonds, pistachios, sesame seeds and lots of sugar go into Moroccan sweets.

hemis.fr/Hughes

DINING OUT

There's more to Moroccan cuisine than couscous. As varied as the country, the food can match any appetite, whether you're in the mood for subtle elegance or hearty peasant fare. The flavours are so subtle you'll have to sit back and analyze them. Beyond the native specialities, in any sizable city you'll find acceptable, often superior, French restaurants. In the north, Spanish cuisine gets special emphasis. If you crave a pizza or a hamburger, this sort of exotica, too, is close at hand.

Breakfast

Some hotels lay on big buffets of hot and cold foods for breakfast—everything from cornflakes to fried eggs with a wide range of home-baked pastries. Other hotels serve a continental breakfast consisting of a croissant and a roll with butter and jam, and coffee, tea or hot chocolate. Whatever the offer, look for the local orange juice, which is wonderfully refreshing.

Moroccan Cuisine

Traditional Moroccan specialities are colourful, spicy and often festive, involving fragrant herbs, vegetables, olives, dried fruit, preserved lemons and sweet peppers. The spices used are flavourful and generally mild—apart

from the little bowl of harissa served with a couscous, a searing paste of chili and garlic, to be taken with caution. The most common spices are cinnamon, cumin, turmeric, ginger, paprika, anise, cloves, coriander, sesame seed, saffron and black pepper. The famous blend known as *ras el hanout* ("the best of the shop") can contain 20 to 30 spices, and perhaps dried rose petals. Rose water and orange flower water are used to flavour desserts.

Starters

Whether you're eating in a fancy restaurant or the most basic café deep in the medina, a great way to start a meal is *harira,* a chickpea soup that really "sticks to your ribs". Depending on the cook or the occasion, it may contain meat chunks, lentils, pumpkin, onions and tomatoes. *Tchoutchouka* is similar to French *ratataouille*, a stew of sweet peppers, tomatoes, garlic and various spices slowly simmered in oil. Pigeon pie, *pastilla*, or *bstilla*, is a festive dish, sometimes the prelude to a banquet, sometimes the centrepiece of the meal. The crust of light flaky pastry encloses a fragrant stuffing of stewed pigeon meat flavoured with ginger and saffron, sprinkled with almonds and a sweet egg-and-herb sauce. Before serving, the top is sprinkled with cinnamon and icing sugar. The sweet-savoury flavour may take you aback at first but it is surprisingly addictive. *Bstilla* can also be made with mushrooms, chicken, quail or seafood.

Tajines
The name comes from the earthenware pot in which the *tajine* is stewed. The recipe can feature lamb, mutton, veal or beef, with a rich supporting cast of potatoes, turnips, courgettes, okra, tomatoes, onions, beans, olives, lemon and herbs and spices. There are fish *tajines,* as well.

Chicken stews come in lavish varieties—in unexpected alliance with olives and lemon or prunes and almonds. The chicken is cooked so slowly it all but drops off the bones.

Couscous
North Africa's most famous dish takes a formidable amount of work to prepare authentically. The semolina has to be subdued into delicate, almost microscopic grains, none mingling in lumps, and steamed, flavoured and re-steamed just so. Lamb, chicken or fish goes on top, with a spicy sauce and potatoes, chickpeas, peppers, tomatoes, courgettes, turnips, pumpkins and raisins.

Mechoui
In your travels you may stumble on a festival at which a whole lamb on a spit is being roasted over the coals. This is *mechoui,* a ceremonial affair so good that it is reproduced at the most expensive tourist banquets. While the meat is being cooked and basted, the aroma sends out enticing signals to the appetite of anyone within range.

Fish and Seafood
The best Atlantic and Mediterranean fish and seafood—from sardines to lobster—grace Moroccan restaurant tables, most commonly along the coasts. Specialist restaurants in the ports provide memorable grilled sea bass, mullet, tuna steaks, prawns, mussels and squid. Look over the day's catch, choose what looks right, then order some fish soup while the cooks go to work.

Desserts

Sweets tend to be very sweet in Morocco, dripping with sugar or honey or both. For some sort of record in sweetness per cubic centimetre, try *dattes farcies,* dates stuffed with marzipan. If you find them too syrupy, there's always fresh fruit to vary the diet: melons, oranges, strawberries, bananas or peaches.

Drinks

Many bars and restaurants in hotels and the *nouvelles villes* are licensed to serve beer, wine and spirits. During the French era, Morocco became a serious wine-producing country and there are very drinkable local vintages—red, white and rosé. Ask the waiter for advice. Locally brewed beer is popular, and cheaper than imported brands. The great majority of Moroccans respect Islam's view about alcoholic drinks. They devote themselves, instead, to round-the-clock consumption of sweet mint tea, as a look at any café terrace will reveal. At its best, with fresh mint floating in the pot, this is a most soothing drink to linger over.

Mint tea must be poured from on high, to create a little foam. | Couscous and all its attendant dishes. | Stewed lamb with prunes and sesame seeds, a rich and tasty combination.

Huber/Fantuz

Huber/Schmid

Huber/Scatà

SPORTS

Making the most of its diversified geography and climate, Morocco has something attractive for sports enthusiasts of every stripe, whether nature-lovers, water-skiers or hikers. For just watching, the great national enthusiasm is football (soccer); Morocco's team is one of the best in Africa.

Windsurfing and sailboarding
Surfers and sailboarders find plenty of challenge in those Atlantic waves. Among the more popular hangouts are Mehdia beach near Kenitra, the Plage des Nations at Rabat, Safi beach, Sidi Kaouki near Essaouira, and many spots near Agadir.

Sailing
Yacht clubs are strung along the coasts all the way from Tangier to Agadir, with a concentration of activities in centres such as Rabat and Casablanca. A few discreet resorts on the Mediterranean coast are worth discovering.

Fishing
Boat trips to rich fishing grounds can be arranged in the principal ports. Professionals in the resorts know when and where the big ones—blue fin tuna, swordfish, barracuda and friends—are waiting to be pulled in.

Lake and river fishing for trout or pike is popular in the Middle Atlas. You have to get a permit from the Direction des Eaux et Forêts, headquartered in Rabat but with offices in all the cities.

Golf
Morocco's most grandiose golf complex is the Royal Golf Dar-es-Salam near Rabat, with courses designed by Robert Trent Jones. Another prestigious place to play is the 18-hole links at Mohammedia.

Mountain-biking
The sport has quickly developed on the tracks and paths of the Atlas mountains. From short rides to circuits of several days, there are plenty of opportunities.

Hiking
All year round, Morocco is the ideal destination for enthusiastic hikers, whether you want to join a

guided group organized by an agency or prefer to do it your own way. The region around Toubkal, the highest point of the Atlas at 4,167 m (13,670 ft) is the most popular, though there are plenty of other suitable areas.

Riding

Equestrian clubs are scattered around the country in towns and resorts. Increasingly popular are organized treks into the Middle Atlas, lasting one day or several.

istockphoto.com/Quillet

Hunting

The Réserve Touristique d'Arba-oua is a happy hunting ground among foreign tourists. Located near Larache in northwestern Morocco, it's available only to non-residents. The marshy plateau is rich in wild boar and bird life. You have to show your national permit to obtain a temporary Moroccan licence.

Skiing

From Fez, Meknès and Marrakesh, the slopes are within easy reach. The most highly developed ski resort in the High Atlas is the Oukaïmeden, at the end of a dependably snow-free road from Marrakesh. The slopes are at an altitude of 2,600 m (8,500 ft). The season usually lasts from December to March. The most popular resort is Michliffen, near Ifrane, at 2,000 m (6,500 ft).

hemis.fr/Frilet

Author's Image

THE HARD FACTS

On the countdown to your trip, here are a few essential points you ought to know about Morocco:

Airports
Casablanca's Mohammed V Airport is the base of the national company, Royal Air Maroc. Thanks to the development of low-cost companies, a dozen other Moroccan airports handle international flights, as well as charter flights. Marrakesh, Agadir, Ouarzazate, Fez and Tangier, among others, are directly linked to several European cities. As a result, most Moroccan airports have been modernized and offer many services including car hire, bureaux de change and tourist information offices.

Car hire
International and local car hire companies compete for customers, and prices are usually reasonable. You can sign up by the day, or for three days, or a week with unlimited mileage included. The minimum age is 21, though some companies draw the line at 25. The easiest way to pay is with a credit card; otherwise you will be required to put down a big cash deposit. Some companies let you pick up the car in one city and return it in another, at no extra cost. Check the contract carefully as many companies will allow only 4x4 vehicles on tracks.

Climate
For the major part of the year, the weather is temperate in most of Morocco. Near the coast the influence of the sea moderates summer heat-waves, and in winter the average temperatures rarely drop below 10°C (50°F). The interior of the country, with a continental climate, is hotter than the coast in summer and colder in winter. It's three times rainier in Tangier than in Agadir. Desert summers are best avoided.

Communications
The Moroccan telephone system is efficient. In all the towns you will have no problem finding a phone booth functioning with coins or cards, and here are numerous téléboutiques. If you take your mobile phone, you can buy a card for a local operator.

Both national and international calls are more expensive in Morocco than in Europe. Big hotels generally have internet services, and there are plenty of Internet cafés.

Mail works relatively eficiently. The PTT sells stamps, as do places that deal in postcards. For fastest processing of your homeward bound postcards, use the post box in the PTT.

Complaints

If you think a taxi driver or a fast-talking salesman in the souk has taken advantage of you, it's probably too late to have the price reduced. In all cases involving money, like hiring a guide or a horse and carriage— avoid the problem by settling on a price beforehand. Otherwise, most problems can be negotiated with a shrug and a smile. In a hotel or restaurant ask to see the manager.

Currency

The unit of currency is the Moroccan *dirham* (DH), divided into 100 *centimes*. In practice, tourists rarely see anything smaller than a half-dirham coin. Coins go up to 10 DH. Banknotes are issued in denominations of 10, 50, 100 and 200 DH.

Well-known credit cards such as MasterCard and Visa are accepted in hotels, restaurants and some shops and there are

plenty of cash distributors. Euros are accepted in some places.

It's best to change travellers cheques at the bank. Always have your passport with you as you will need to give proof of your identity whenever you want to change money. Always have some small change handy for tips.

Driving

The roads are generally good, and the motorway network (tolled) is being expanded. But the local standard of driving—and walking, too—means you can never relax your vigilance.

The regulations resemble those of France; direction signs are normally written in French as well as Arabic. Speed limits are normally 40 km per hour in towns and 100 km per hour on the highway. Other than the unpredictable human element, such as country folk and livestock meandering down the middle of a highway, the dangers include the weather. Tracks *(pistes)* in mountain and desert regions can be flooded by melting snow or sudden rainstorms, and accumulations of snow can snarl the mountain roads between November and springtime.

Night driving in general can be very dangerous, with unlit bicycles, animals, potholes and other surprises potentially around every bend. Pleasant tree-shaded rest areas with picnic tables are frequently found along the highways; they are sign-posted *"Aire de repos"* well in advance.

In and around the towns there are plenty of petrol stations to choose from but be sure to fill up before undertaking any wilderness jaunts. (Stations supplying lead-free petrol are rare but well signposted.)

Drugs

If you are offered *kif,* the highly regarded local hashish, be very prudent; some dealers are reputed to be police informers, and penalties can be stiff.

Essentials

Just about anything you might need can be bought on the spot in Morocco, but if you require prescription drugs be sure to carry your own. A comprehensive first-aid kit is good to have, and don't forget insect repellent and sunscreen cream.

As for clothing, remember that nights are chilly in the desert and the mountains. For Morocco's conservative environment you'll need very modest styles; "revealing" fashions are okay in a resort hotel but not in a remote village.

Formalities

For most tourists no visa is required to enter Morocco; all you need is a valid passport, unless you want to stay more than three months.

Adults may bring into Morocco 200 cigarettes or 50 cigars or 400 g tobacco and one litre each of wine and spirits, and 5 g perfume. It's forbidden to import or export the national currency, the *dirham.* You can bring in as much foreign currency as you wish but any amounts exceeding the equivalent of 15,000 DH must be declared. Change it into dirhams a bit at a time, according to need. You are supposed to change your unused dirhams into foreign currency before leaving the country, but only 50 per cent of the amount exchanged on arrival can be re-exchanged if you have stayed longer than 48 hours.

Health

No special inoculations are required for visiting Morocco. Consult your doctor in case he recommends topping up the shots you may have had for previous trips, especially if you'll be travelling in the south. A travel health insurance policy is a wise investment before you leave home. On the spot, avoid too much sun; start with morning and late afternoon outings, and splash on the sunscreen lotion. It's prudent to drink mineral water and avoid dubious food stalls. If the worst happens, any pharmacy will dole out pills to hurry you back to health. In case you need a doctor, the pharmacy, your hotel or your consulate can recommend one.

Water is generally fit to drink and can be quite delicious, being filtered by the Atlas mountains but to be on the safe side, especially in the south, stick to bottled mineral water or the national standby, mint tea.

Holidays and festivals

Because two calendars are used in Morocco—the standard Gregorian model of 365 days as well as the Muslim year, which is 11 days shorter—things tend to be complicated. New Year's Day, a national holiday, always falls on January 1, but religious holidays follow a different rhythm. Consequently there's no such thing as a religious holiday that always occurs at a certain season.

Here is the line-up of non-religious public holidays:

January 1	New Year
May 1	Labour Day
July 9	Youth Day
July 30	Fête du Trône (Coronation of Mohammed VI)
August 14	Allegiance Day
November 6	Anniversary of the Green March
November 18	Independence Day

Media

Moroccan dailies are published in Arabic, French and Spanish. British and European newspapers and the *International Herald Tribune* are sold at news kiosks in all the big cities.

In addition to Moroccan television, in Arabic and French, many hotels provide satellite service, relaying programmes from French, Italian, German and English-language networks.

No entry

If you are non-Muslim you will not be allowed to enter the prayer halls of mosques in Morocco. However, you can get a peek into some of the most impressive ones. Among the few places excepted from the no-go rule are the Mohammed V mausoleum in Rabat and the sanctuary of Moulay Ismaïl in Meknès.

Opening hours

Most administrative offices are open from 8.30 a.m. to noon and from 2.30 to 6.30 p.m., with a longer break on Fridays in deference to midday prayers.

Banks open Monday to Friday from 8.30 a.m. to 12.30 p.m. and again from 2 to 6.30 p.m. Bureaux de change in touristic areas keep more flexible hours.

Main post offices are open from 8 a.m. to 6.30 p.m. Monday to Thursday; Fridays it's 8 a.m. to noon and 4 p.m. to 6.30 p.m. Summer hours are curtailed.

Shops in the medinas tend to operate from 8 a.m. to 9 p.m. daily, with a Friday break for prayers. In the *nouvelles villes,* a daily siesta from about noon to 3 p.m. is standard.

Museums follow an erratic schedule but most take a midday break.

During Ramadan, all these times change, and work generally starts earlier, around 8 a.m., to finish at 3 p.m. or 4 p.m.

Photography

Be prepared for wide variations in exposure, from the deep shadows of the kasbah to the blinding reflection of sun on the white houses. You don't have to speak the language to ask someone's permission before taking a picture. Taking photos of women, in particular, can be a sensitive matter. Sensitive, too, are military installations, ports and airports, where photography is forbidden. Make sure you take several spare memory cards, and don't forget the battery charger.

Police

Municipal police, who direct traffic, will be helpful and courteous if you need directions. The Sûreté Nationale fights crime in towns and also patrols the highways. Another police organization, the

Gendarmerie, deals with security and operates roadblocks in sensitive areas.

In much of the country, the telephone number for emergency police business is 19.

Safety

Carrying whopping bankrolls or flashy jewellery only tempts fate. Keep valuables in your hotel safe. Leave nothing of value in a car, visible or hidden, locked or unlocked. In crowded markets and terminals beware of pickpockets.

Social graces

Moroccans are friendly and open with visitors. Much hand-shaking goes on, but that's about as much formality as you're liable to meet. You shouldn't be too polite; for instance, a waiter might be offended to be called "sir" or thanked too effusively.

If you can learn a few elementary phrases in Arabic you'll be rewarded with surprised smiles and kindnesses.

Taxis

Petits taxis, small cars with rooftop luggage racks, take up to three passengers on trips within cities (and up to 10 km or 6 miles beyond). Most have meters. For longer distances, or excursions, choose a more spacious *grand taxi*, but negotiate the price.

Time

All of Morocco is on Greenwich Mean Time (GMT), putting the clocks forward an hour for summer time (re-introduced experimentally in 2008).

Tipping

People often let you know, subtly or otherwise, when a tip is appropriate. Don't forget waiters in cafés and restaurants, porters in hotels and terminals, toilet attendants, taxi drivers, helpful museum curators, and (not at all optional) those human parking meters, *gardiens de voitures.*

Toilets

Your best bet is to take advantage of the facilities just off the foyer in any medium or luxury hotel. There are also public conveniences in airports, railway stations, restaurants and cafés.

It's considered the minimum courtesy to invest in a mint tea or a drink if you're using the toilet in a café. Experienced travellers always carry their own toilet paper.

Touts

Although the creation of a tourist police diminished the problem, there are still so-called "false guides", touts and hustlers in all the places that tourists congregate, especially towns like Marrakesh, Fez, Meknes and Agadir. Try to say "no" with a smile, and don't get flustered; say you already have a guide or that you can manage on your own. The word "police" might have a positive effect. If ever you get really lost, ask any friendly-looking child to lead you back to civilization.

Transport

ONCF, l'Office National des Chemins de Fer, runs a comprehensive train service among most of the main Moroccan cities. The busiest line is the TNR (rapid shuttles) between Casablanca and Rabat, with frequent, speedy trains and a comfort level in 2nd class up to European standards.

Luxury coaches with air-conditioning roll along the highways between all the principal cities; regional buses are slower and less comfortable.

Voltage

The standard is 220-volt A.C., with French-style plugs. But some towns are still on 110-volt power, so you'd better ask.

Women Travellers

Women travelling alone are often approached and followed around by young Moroccan men in the most touristic areas. Normally this does not pose a threat, but wearing modest clothing and using a minimum of common sense will also help.

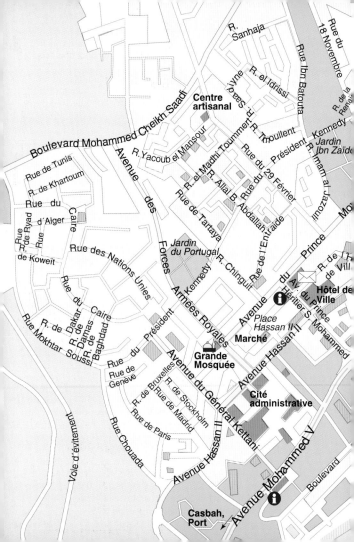

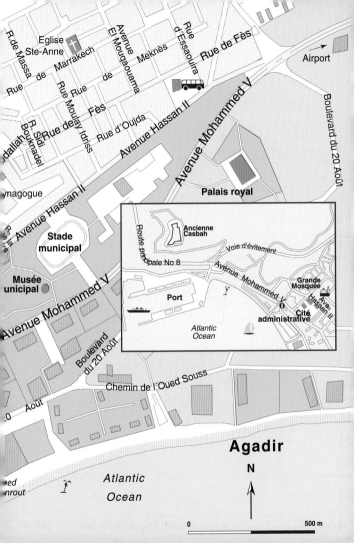

Agadir

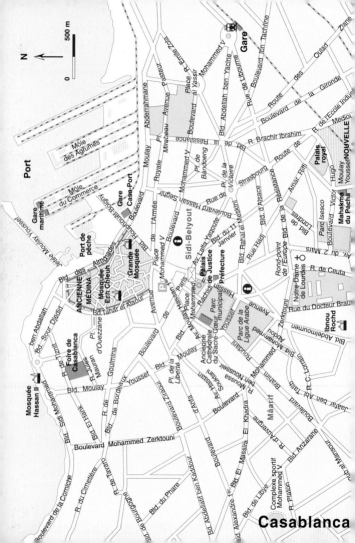

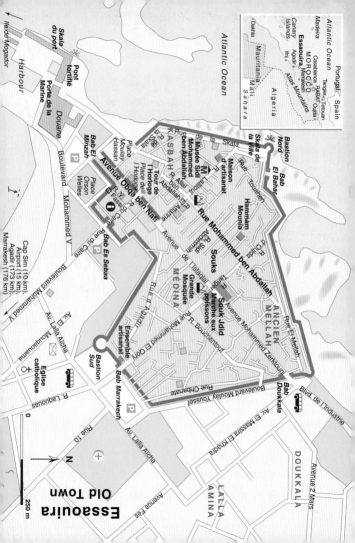

Essaouira Old Town

250 m

N

0

Atlantic Ocean

Portugal Spain
Madeira
Atlantic Ocean
Casablanca RABAT Oujda
Tanger, Tetuan
MOROCCO
Canary Agadir **Essaouira, Marrakesh**
Islands Ifni
Dakhla Atlas Mountains
Mali Algeria
Mauritania
W e s t e r n   S a h a r a

Île de Mogador
Harbour
Skala du port
Pont fortifié
Porte de la Marine
Douane
Boulevard Mohammed V
Bastion Nord
Bab El Bahar
Skala de la Ville
Rue de la Skala
Rue Touahen
Maison d'artisanat
Rue de la Skala
KASBAH
Place Moulay Hassan
Musée Sidi Mohammed ben Abdallah
Rue Mohammed ben Abdallah
Avenue l'Istiqlal
Tour de l'Horloge
Place de l'Horloge
Rue Ibn Rochd
Hammam Mounia
Rue Mohammed ben Abdallah
Souks
Avenue de l'Istiqlal
Souk Jdid
Avenue Mohammed Zerktouni
Grande Mosquée
Marché aux poissons
Rue El Mellah
ANCIEN MELLAH
MÉDINA
Rue Attarine
Rue Mohammed El Qorry
Rue Sidi Abdesmih
Rue du Caire
Avenue Oqba ben Nafi
Bab El Minzah
Bab Es Sebaa
Place Orson Welles
Bab Marrakech
Ensemble artisanal
Bastion Sud
Rue Chbanate
Boulevard Moulay Youssef
Rue R. Bouchentouf
Av. El Massira El Khadra
Bab Doukkala
Blvd. de l'Industrie
DOUKKALA
LALLA AMINA
Avenue 2 Mars
Av. Lalla Aicha
Avenue Fès
Rue 10
R. Lagunas
Av. Lalla Aicha
Église catholique
Boulevard Mohammed V
Mohammed V
Av. Moqaouama
Cap Sim (10 km);
Airport (15 km);
Agadir (173 km);
Marrakesh (176 km)

P
P
P
P

i

Meknès

0   300 m

N

CASBAH HEDRACHE

Jardins de l'École d'Horticulture

Bab en Nouara

Oued Boufekrane

Heri es Souani

Dar el Ma

BENI M'HAMMED

Bassin de l'Agdal

Aguedal des Riches

Bab el Khan

VIEUX MEKRA

Bab el Khan

Boulevard Abderrahmane ben Zidane

Méchouar

Dar el Makhzen Palais royal

VILLE IMPÉRIALE

Bori el Ma

(Ancien jardin des Sultanes)

Golf royal

Cimetière musulman

SIDI AMAR HASSINI

Bab el Hri

Mausolée de Moulay Ismail

DAR KEBIRA

Koubbet el Khiyatin

VIEUX MEKRA

Centre Mansour artisanal

Bab el Hedim

Place Lalla Aouda

Gare routière

Boulevard Bou Ameïr

Rue Rouamzine

Avenue des Forces Armées Royales

Rue Bir Anzarane

Hôpital Moulay Ismail

Avenue Bou Ameïr

Rue des Moulins

Dar Jamaï (Musée des Arts marocains)

Palais el Mansour

Grande Mosquée

Médersa Bou Inania

Kissaria

MEDINA

Jama ez Zitouna

Rue Souïka

Boulevard el Haboul

Jardin el Haboul

Bab Tizimi

Palais de Justice

Carrefour Moulay Ismaïl

Piscine

Av. 11 Janvier

Route de Rabat

Pl. Administrative Av. Idriss II

Hôtel de Ville

Av. Mohammed V

Bd. ben Abdellah

R. d'Accra

R. de Paris

Av. des Forces Armées Royales

Bd.-el-Mouahidine

R. Moulay Abou Chaïb

R. Moulay Abdelaziz

R. Sebou

R. Oumn el Moukhtar

R. Tahar Hachemad

R. Meknès

R. Ferhat Hachemad

Mosquée el Berdaïne

Pl. Berdaïne

Boulevard Circulaire

VILLE NOUVELLE

Place Abdelaziz ben Idriss

R. Moulay Halid

Rue Ali ben Roussel

Avenue Yougoslavia

R-Ogba ben Nafaa

Av. el Adaabi

R. Mansour

R. Ferhat Hachemad

R. El Menhithine

Stade municipal

R. al Andalous

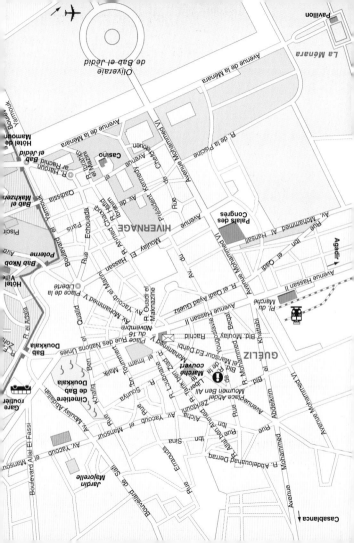

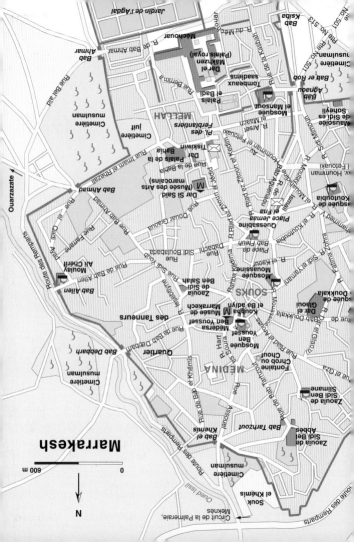

Agadir 51-52, 73
Aïn Diab 14-15
Aït Benhaddou 55
Akka 61
Al Hoceïma 52
Alnif 57
Amazrou 59-60
Amtoudi 61
Argan trees 51
Art 68
Asilah 23
Boumalne du Dadès 56
Casablanca 13-15
Cap Spartel 20-21
Ceuta 23
Chaouen 23, 73
Chellah 17
Dadès Valley 55-57
Desert 63-67
Drâa Valley 59
El Jadida 49, 52
El Kelaa des M'Gouna 56
El Mansour dam 56
Er Rachidia 57
Erfoud 57
Erg Chebbi 58
Essaouira 49-51
Fez 28-31
Fint 58-59
Goulimine 61, 73
Hammam 68
Islam 68-69
Jorf 57
Languages 69
Lixus 16, 23
Markets 73
Marrakesh 33-47, 73
Djemaa el Fna 33-34
Gardens 45-47
Kasbah 39-44
New Town 44-47
Palm Grove 47

Meknès 25-26
Melilla 23
Merzouga 58
Meski 57
Mhamid 60
Michliffen 79
Mohammedia 52
Moulay Idriss 26
Moussem 69
Music 69
Oases 63-66
Oualidia 52x
Ouarzazate 55-56, 73
Oukaïmeden 47
Ourika Valley 47
Ouzoud Falls 47
Rabat 15-17
Ramadan 69
Rissani 57-58, 73
Safi 49
Salé 17
Setti Fatma 47
Skoura 56
Tafilalt 57-58
Tafraoute 52
Taliouine 60
Tamegroute 60
Tangier 19-21
Taorirt, kasbah 55-56
Taroudant 55-56
Tata 60-61
Tazzarine 57
Tetouan 21-23
Tinerhir 56
Tinfou 60
Tinzouline 61
Tiznit 73
Todra Gorges 56
Valley of Roses 56
Volubilis 16, 26-28
Zagora 59, 73
Souks 35-36

General editor
Barbara Ender-Jones

Oases and Desert
Michel Puységur
and Judith Farr

Design
Karin Palazzolo

Layout
Luc Malherbe
Matias Jolliet

Photo credits
p. 1: hemis.fr/Giuglio
p. 2: istockphoto.com/Seidl (lamp);
hemis.fr/Wysocki (kasbah Aït Arbi);
hemis.fr/Giuglio (tea);
Barbara Ender (spices)

Maps
JPM Publications,
Mathieu Germay

Copyright © 2009, 1994
JPM Publications S.A.
12, avenue William-Fraisse,
1006 Lausanne, Switzerland
information@jpmguides.com
http://www.jpmguides.com/

Printed in Switzerland
12840-00-4994
Weber Benteli/Bienne
Edition 2009

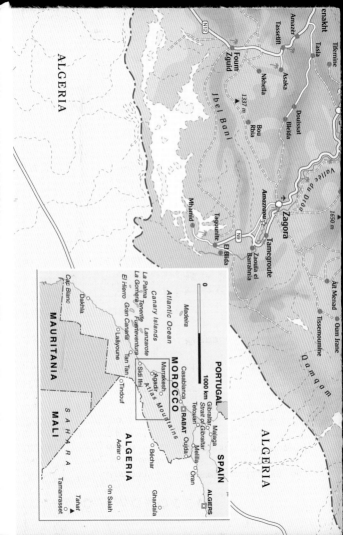

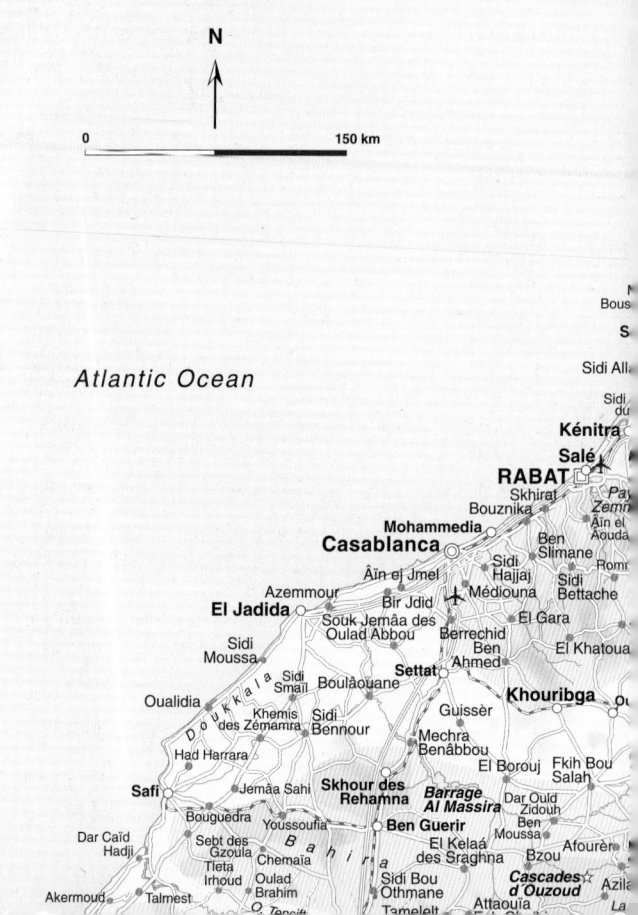

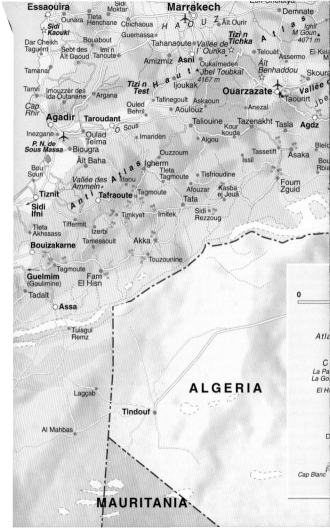

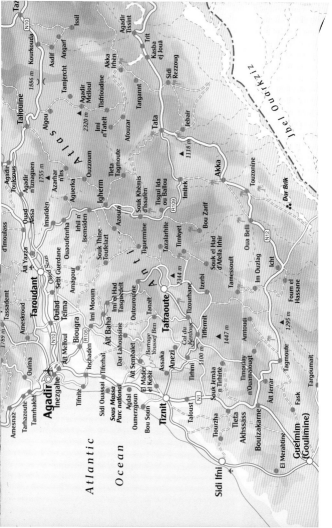

SPAIN

Cádiz
Málaga

Spain
Morocco
Algeciras Gibraltar
Tarifa
Strait of Gibraltar
Monte Hacho
Tanger
Grottes d'Hercule
Ksar es Seghir
Ceuta
Smir Restinga
Cabo Negro
Martil
El Fendek
Dar Ben Karriche
Tétouan

Mediterranean Sea

Asilah
El Bahri
Souk el Arba des Beni Hassan
Bou Ahmed
El Jebha
Al Hoceima
Cap Ras Tarf
Cap des Trois Fourches
Melilla
Beni Enzar
Nador
Segangane
Driouch

Lixus
Larache
Chaouen
Pays Rhomara
Bni
Boufrah
Ketama
Targuist
Tizirhine
Kassita
Midar
Zaïo

Ksar el Kebir
Bab Taza
RIF
M. Tidiquin
2448 m
Boured
Aknoul
Saka
Melga el Ouidane

Moulay Bousselham
Arbaoua
Mokrisset
Ouazzane
Zoumi
Tahar Souk
Taïneste
Mezguitem
Taourirt

Souk el Arba du Rharb
El Tazi
Had Kourt
Fès el Bali
Rhafsaï
Ourtzarh
Taounate
Aïn Aïcha

Yahya el Rharb
Sidi Slimane
Sidi Kacem
O. Ouerrha
Karia Ba Mohamed
O. Sebou
Tissa
Sidi Abdallah des Rhiata
Taza
Msoun
Guercif

Forêt de la Maâmora
Dar Bel Amri
Volubilis
CHERAGA
Fès
Jbel Tazzeka
Debdou

Sidi Allal el Bahraoui
Tiflet
Moulay Idriss
Meknès
Sidi Harazem

Khemisset
Boufakrane
El Menzel
Berkine
O. Moulouya

Mâaziz
Tiddas
El Harcha
Oulmès
El Hajeb
Sefrou
Tazouta
Tamjilt
Meski
Plateau du Rekkam

Ez Zhiliga
Ito
Azrou
Ifrane
Aïn Leuh
Mrirt
Forêt de Cèdres
Boulemane
Enjil
Oulad Ali
J. Bou Naceur
3340 m
Tissaf
Matarka

Khénifra
Timahdite
Sources de l'Oum er Rbia
Moyen - Atlas
Missour
Outat Oulad El Haj
Ouizrhet

Oued Zem
Boujad
El Kebab
Itzèr
Boulôjoul
Anoual

Kasba Tadla
Ouaou mana
El Ksiba
Boumia
Midelt
Azdad
Talsinnt

Beni Mellal
Jbel Masker
3277 m
Jbel Ayachi
3737 m
Cirque de Jaffar
Gourrama
Mellaha
Jbel Khang el Ghar
Borj Tajjite
Borj Bassia

Bin el Ouidane
Imilchil
Haut - Atlas
Rich
Gorges du Ziz
Bouânane

Cathédrale
Agoudal
Aït
Er Rachidia

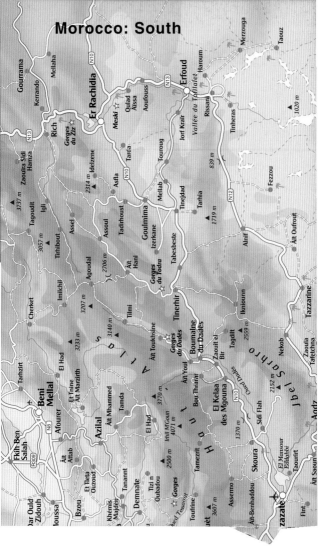

Morocco: South